THE SUFFOLK COUNTY SCANDALS INVESTIGATIONS
A REMINESCENCE

WILLIAM F. F. YOUNG

Outskirts Press, Inc.
Denver, Colorado

To

Ellen and Joseph

Also by William F. F. Young

Thomas E. Dewey, et al.

Table of Contents

Chapter 1

From its western end, Long Island extends eastward about 120 miles from Long Island City, which is just barely separated from the island of Manhattan by the East River. Kings County and Queens County, the two most westerly of the four counties situate on Long Island, are two of the five counties constituting the City of New York. Kings County is the New York City borough of Brooklyn; Queens, the borough of Queens. Kings County forms the southwestern end of Long Island, and is bordered on the north and east by Queens County, the easterly line of which is the westerly line of Nassau County. Travelling eastward through some fifteen miles of Nassau County brings one to the westerly line of Suffolk County.

The 922 square miles of Suffolk County, the second largest county in the state of New York, are distributed among ten towns. At the western end of the county, bordered on the north by Long Island Sound, is the Town of Huntington, below which, running to the south shore and the Atlantic Ocean, is the Town of Babylon. To the east of Huntington on the north shore is the Town of Smithtown; and below Smithtown is the Town of Islip, which extends to the south shore. To the east of Smithtown and Islip is the Town of Brookhaven, the largest township in the state, which runs from shore to shore, and which is larger than the whole of Nassau County. East of Brookhaven are the Town of Riverhead (the hamlet of Riverhead is the county seat), bordered on the north by Long Island Sound, and on the south by the Town of Southhampton, which is bordered on the south by the Atlantic Ocean. From the easternmost juncture of the towns of Riverhead and Southampton, the county splits into what are referred to as the North and South Forks. East of Riverhead on the North Fork is the Town of Southold, which extends to Orient Point, at the northeasterly tip of Long Island. East of Southampton is the Town of East Hampton, which extends to Montauk Point. Early and mid-19th century whalers sailed to the ends of the earth from Sag Harbor, situate in both the towns of Southampton and East Hampton. Also in East Hampton is Amagansett, which, in the small hours of June 12, 1942, was the site of the only landing of foreign forces in the United State since the War of 1812, when four operatives of the German Secret Service, transported by submarine, disembarked there. The tenth town is Shelter Island, an islet lying between the North and South Forks, bounded by Shelter Island Sound and Gardiners Bay.

It wasn't until just before the turn of the twentieth century that the counties of New York, Bronx, Richmond, Queens and Kings were consolidated by the state legislature to form New York City. As part of that process, the three easternmost towns of Queens County were lopped off to form Nassau County.

Suffolk County goes back to Colonial times. The county was originally known as the East Riding of the Province of Yorkshire. The Province of Yorkshire was the name for all of what was to become the State of New York, a patent for all of which Charles II had granted to his brother, the Duke of York, in May of 1664. In September of that year, Peter Stuyvesant finally surrendered Manhattan Island, the symbol of the Dutch in New York, to the Duke. When the East Riding became a county in 1683 by order of the first New York Colonial Legislature, the whole county accounted for less than 2,000 people.

At the beginning of the twentieth century, there were less than 80,000 residents of Suffolk County. In 1910, with a population of 96,000, it was still essentially rural when the Pennsylvania Railroad put into operation its tunnels under the East River, thus enabling its Long Island Railroad to carry its passengers in and out of Manhattan. Until this underwater connection was effected, Long Island-Manhattan travellers had to take the ferry back and forth across the East River between Long Island City and Manhattan. The new direct link with New York City made possible the Long Island commuter.

By 1920, the county's population had risen to 110,000. By 1930, the number of commuters other than the wealthy and well-to-do had become significant, and the county's population had risen to 161,000. Its beaches on the Atlantic Ocean on its south shore, and on Long Island Sound on its north shore had made Suffolk County attractive as a summer sanctuary for a fairly wide financial range of non-residents as far back as the late 1800's. More recently, the county had become a magnet for the wealthy. In between the Nassau-Suffolk line on the West, and Orient Point and Montauk Point on the East, both shores had countless expensive homes and some truly magnificent estates.

In the Town of Huntington, there was the 1,355-acre Lloyd's Harbor manor of Marshall Field III, which included, in addition to the 57-room main house, numerous smaller residential structures, polo grounds, a fresh water lake, a game preserve, and twenty-five miles of its own roads. Also in Huntington was the forty-three acre summer establishment of William K. Vanderbilt II at Centerport, which, in addition to a mansion featuring columns from the ruins of Carthage, included a museum memorializing Commodore Vanderbilt's world travels. At the eastern end of the county, there was a long-established concentration of the extremely well-to-do in the Hamptons. The shores of Suffolk County, like the Manhattan economic oases of Park and Fifth Avenues and Central Park West, had a significant number of people whose notably comfortable way of life was not affected by the Depression.

In the late 1930's, the windows in the schools throughout the county were still the huge kind that required a long pole with a hook at one end to unlock or latch them where the sashes met, or to pull down the bottom sash if it was open all the way. High street curbs were still in the process of being lowered. In Huntington, the doctors, who had been charging two dollars for house calls as well as for office visits, had just recently decided the traffic might bear three dollars for house calls. Many of the doctors throughout the county, particularly those in the eastern towns, were still taking their fees in farm produce, and those who were renting sometimes paid part of their rent with it. Some of them could not have survived if it had not been for the patients they treated at the expense of the county's welfare department. As for the lawyers, even though their number was small, a good many of them were barely getting by.

By 1940, there were 197,000 people living in Suffolk County. Most of its population was in its five western towns; and many of the wage earners in the western towns were commuters. There was still little manufacturing or other industrial activity of any consequence. The commerce was still mainly that of the local small businessman; and there were still a lot of farmers working a lot of farmland. Even in the most westerly part of the county, which is to say that part of the county closest to Nassau County--and, by extension, the part of it nearest New York City--one could drive through large areas in which what one saw mostly were potatoes and cabbages; and as one drove eastward toward the county seat and then past it onto the North Fork, that would seem to be about all one could see.

———— ◆ ————

Throughout the United States during the Depression, there had been very little money in circulation, the birth rate had been low, and there had been very little home construction. During the Second World War, although there were significant housing shortages around the country consequent to the wartime dislocations of civilian life, there still was no homebuilding going on, because just about all the materials one needed in order to construct a house were declared to be war-essential.

Following the end of the war in 1945, an upswing in the marriage and birth rates compounded the problem; and there was a monumental housing shortage across the country. When the nationwide demand for housing was coupled with the enactment of the mortgage-loan entitlement part of the G.I. Bill of Rights and a significant expansion of the Federal Housing Administration mortgage guarantee program, a vast market for new homes came into being, resulting in an historic broadening of the country's home-owning base.

In New York City, there simply were not enough habitable apartments for people of limited means. The advent of the G.I. mortgage and the increased availability of the FHA mortgage made it possible for young couples who could afford only moderate apartment rentals to own their own homes. (In Nassau and Suffolk Counties, in those days of 4% 30-year GI mortgages and school-district taxes that had not yet begun to mushroom, the new homeowners' monthly payments to the bank, which included the monthly portion of their tax and house insurance bills, as well as their principal and interest payments, could wind up being less than the rent they would have had to pay for something much less desirable in a city apartment.) When, in addition to the unavailability of housing in the city and the availability of home financing for people who had litle in the bank, the city dwellers considered all the positive things about not having to live in the city and all the good things about being able to live in areas which were relatively close in distance and time from the city, where almost all of them worked, they decided *en masse* to become home-owners in the suburbs.

Suburbs--residential areas on the outskirts of cities-- are said to have existed in Mesopotamia as far back as 2000 B.C. Chaucer refers to them in *The Canterbury Tales*. We are told that in 1665, the plague, and then in 1666, fire gave impetus to the growth of the suburbs of London. In America, the suburbs around the hubs of Boston, New York and Philadelphia go back to pre-Revolutionary times. The first notable instance of the magical combination of pastoral residential atmosphere and easy access to an urban business center in the United States was Brooklyn Heights, just across New York Harbor from Manhattan, in the early 1800's.[1]

In the case of Long Island, i.e., Nassau and Suffolk Counties, at the beginning, most of the post-World War II settlers had lived and worked in New York City, and had resided in either Queens or Brooklyn. They were people who had decided, on the basis of their ages, their children's ages, the availability of VA and FHA financing, and the long-term appeal of a present residence as an attractive place in which they might also like to live in retirement, and the indisputable appeal of "the country" as a place in which to live and bring up their children, that moving out of the city and into the country was the thing to do. They were people who decided, with the help of the necessary rationalizing, that it wouldn't cost anymore anyhow-- the breadwinner would simply commute by train or by car to and from his place of work.

It was in Nassau County that, starting in 1947 on some 4,000 acres of potato farms in the Town of Hempstead, Levitt and Sons began the construction of a residential development initially named

Island Trees. When completed in 1951, by which time the development was known as Levittown, it numbered 17,447 homes, the largest number of homes constituting a single community ever built in this country by a single builder. The reason for the initial lead taken by Nassau County in the growth of suburbia on Long Island may have been that the wish to flee the city for the suburbs was tempered by the normal human instinct not to stray too far from one's home base, even if one's home base--New York City--was not a place where one wanted to stay. In large part, the early post-war residential development of Nassau County may also have reflected the fact that at the beginning of the post-war wave of urban immigrants, the vast majority of them had to work in the city. (Levittown was only twenty-five miles from Manhattan.) It was not until the 1950's that any sizeable portion of the new residents other than doctors and dentists could find sufficient employment where they lived, because the expansion of the local employment market required a sizeable number of new residents to be in place before the existing local businesses could expand and new ones develop. Eventually, as commercial and industrial users of land concluded that they would be much better off if their existing businesses and proposed business ventures were located not in any part of the city but anywhere that was out of it, the industrial and commercial development of our county, like that of Nassau County, developed independently of the fact of the greatly increased residential population, although the increasing presence of greater numbers of inhabitants insured a broad, growing and stable pool of employees.

By 1950, Suffolk County's population had risen to 276,000; and by the end of 1955, it was estimated to have reached something more than 412,000. In 1957, a special census would reveal that the population had almost doubled since 1950, having reached 528,000, with the most dramatic increases having occurred in the five western towns. Suffolk County was now the fastest growing county in the country.

———•◆•———

As for the Republican Party in Suffolk County, we held all the county-wide elective offices, the Congressional seat for the county, and all the county's seats in the State legislature. Of equal if not greater importance for the organization, we held seven out of the ten town supervisorships following the 1953 election; and eight of them, following the 1955 and 1957 elections. A supervisor of a town is the counterpart of a mayor of a city. The town supervisors were *ex officio* the county's board of supervisors, the governing body of the county since colonial times, which made all appointments to non-elective county positions that were not controlled by elected departmental officials, such as the county clerk and the county treasurer. In addition, we usually controlled the town boards even in those towns in which we did not have the supervisorships. In short, we controlled everything on the county level, and most of everything on the town level.

Uninterruptedly for a quarter of century, and more or less continuously before that, one could pretty much look at his progress or ascent in the Republican Party in our county as a predictor of his success in terms of appointive or elective office. Our pluralities in the town elections, which were run in the odd-numbered years, and in those for the county-wide offices when they occurred in odd-numbered years, did not have the benefit of the large voter turnout that the county's basic and strong Republican orientation on state and national issues produced in the even numbered years, and were therefore smaller than those which would be expected in the gubernatorial, to say nothing of the presidential elections. Still, if you were nominated, you would be elected, except in the cases of a few situations of Democratic town office holders of long and personal standing in the smaller, usually eastern towns, and by a comfortable margin.

But then, on November 3, 1959, we lost control of the County Board of Supervisors for the first time since 1933, winning only four of the ten town supervisorships, and losing other town elective offices across the county. By the time the polls closed that Tuesday, we had lost control over a massive amount of patronage. A number of party stalwarts of long standing in elective and appointive offices would be out of jobs come the first of January, 1960; and a good many of our people in subordinate positions in the former officials' offices would lose their jobs, since although everyone who worked for a town or the county was included in the state civil service system for certain purposes, such as retirement, hardly any of them were covered for the purposes of tenure. And so, in all the towns in which the positions of Superintendent of Highways, Town Clerk, Assessor of Taxes and Collector of Taxes had been won by the other side, those new town officers could hire and fire at will--just as we always had been able to do. The fact that we were able to retain the countywide offices of Sheriff, District Attorney, County Clerk, and Surrogate was of little consolation.

In addition, there was the unsettling realization that the Democrats' ability to put a lot of their people in office for the first time in over a quarter of a century necessarily had to serve to increase the vigor, optimism and tenacity with which they would strive for political office in the future.

———— ◆ ————

The genesis of the debacle occurred on January 1, 1955, when, for the first time since Herbert H. Lehman was sworn in for his fourth term as Governor on New Year's Day of 1938, a Democrat was installed in the Governor's mansion in Albany. The Democrats immediately set about to attempt to solve a problem of critical importance and long term implications.

The problem was the considerable and steadily increasing statewide electoral significance of post-World War II suburbia, which had mushroomed in traditionally Republican counties, and the concomitant decrease in the statewide electoral significance of New York City, which was historically and overwhelmingly Democratic. In 1938, the total vote for Governor in Suffolk County was 75,000; and in 1954, just under 133,000. In 1938, the Republican percentage of the vote was about 65%. In 1954, notwithstanding the large numbers of new residents from heavily Democratic counties of New York City, the percentage was about 70%. In 1944, New York City cast 54 per cent of the total state vote; but in 1954, its share was only 44 percent.

Unfortunately for the Democrats, they could not increase their vote in New York City, because the city's population was not growing as fast as that of the rest of the state. The only way for them to survive and prosper was to reduce the Republican pluralities in upstate New York, which was mostly and heavily Republican, and in the strongly Republican counties surrounding New York City.[2] It was perfectly clear to both parties that the suburban vote, approaching twice its pre-World War II size, could decide how the state's electoral votes would go in a presidential election, and which party would capture the Governor's mansion and the state's seats in the United States Senate.

Since the prospects for increasing the Democratic plurality in New York City were nil, the only alternative route to increasing the statewide Democratic vote was to diminish the Republican pluralities outside of New York City.[3] This dictated concentrating on upstate New York (with the exception of Albany County, a Democratic stronghold since 1921), and especially on the suburban counties adjacent to New York City, the massive and continuing immigration to which seemed to be increasing the normally Republican pluralities in those counties. Analyses of the voting patterns of suburbia suggested that most of the newer residents of the suburbs were voting Republican, although not to the same extent as the older residents. It was thought by some that the suburban Republican vote had increased in part because a majority of the former New York City residents may have been Republican to begin with. Support for this hypothesis could be found in reduced post-war Republican shares of the New York City vote except in such issue-dominated national elections as 1946 and 1952. There was also the simpler explanation that a significant number of people who voted Democratic when they lived in New York City simply started voting Republican because they were now in suburbia.

The problem was, how were the Democrats to demonstrate to all these people who were voting Republican that they should vote Democratic? The problem is a perennial one for the party out of power, because in most cases, whether the election be town or city, county, state or national, it is not possible to differentiate between the in's and the out's on any objective basis referable to quality of governance; and if you can't demonstrate that your people would be any better than those presently in office, then the only way to win is to show that they're worse than you are. Your people may not be distinguishable from any other group of people who would rather not have to work in the cannery, but you may be able to activate in a selective way the voters' quiescent resentment of people who they feel earn a living without working for a living, which is to say, politicians. You can attempt to demonstrate that the party in power is corrupt; and the Democrats, having won the Governorship in 1954, ultimately would persuade enough voters that we were corrupt and should be turned out of office to bring about precisely that result in 1959. Their accomplishment was not diminished by the fact that in the initiation of their effort they were somewhat indebted to the person who was totally in charge of the Republican Party in the State of New York from 1943 to 1955--or by the fact that we did help them a little.

Notes

1. Kenneth T. Jackson, *Crabgrass Frontier* (New York, Oxford University Press, 1985) 12, 13, 27-28.
2. Leo Egan, "Shapiro Inquiries Looking For Other G.O.P. Counties, *New York Times*, February 13, 1956.
3. Ibid.

Chapter 2

In the futile attempt to fulfill his 1938 and 1942 gubernatorial campaign promises to destroy the Albany Democratic political machine of Dan O'Connell, Thomas E. Dewey, in his first term as Governor, would furnish a notable example of the use of the criminal process as a weapon in political warfare.[1]

Although this required Dewey to take the first steps in his offensive against O'Connell that were visible to the public (the appointment of an Extraordinary Special and Trial Term of the Supreme Court, and the designations of the Supreme Court Justice to preside at it and the Special Prosecutor for it)[2], his actions as Governor were but the fulfillment of his vigorously stated campaign promises, and would be so viewed.

However, as part of his ultimate response to the somewhat unflattering implications of testimony before the United States Senate Crime Investigating Committee, under the chairmanship of Senator Estes Kefauver, in 1951, Governor Dewey would bring about the creation of the New York State office of Commissioner of Investigation, which would make available to the Democrats, the next time they won the Governorship, a public office which, "[a]t the direction of the governor", was to investigate, among other things, "Any matter concerning the faithful execution or effective enforcement of the laws of the state."[3] A finding of misfeasance or nonfeasance by the Commissioner would, of course, make the Governor's appointment of an Extraordinary Special and Trial Term of the Supreme Court for the county involved an appropriate if not an obligatory exercise of his authority as Governor. The beauty of this office for a state administration interested in waging political war via the criminal process was that it was certainly more likely than not that the public would view the appointment of an Extraordinary Special and Trial Term of the Supreme Court for the county which had been targeted not as a political initiative of the Governor, but rather as his responding appropriately to the findings of an independent office of state government. The fact that under the statute creating the office of Commissioner of Investigation, the Commissioner could embark upon his investigations only "at the direction the governor" would not be articulated in the reportage of the Commissioner's endeavors.

It came about in this way.

On March 12, 1951, the Kefauver Committee opened its public hearings in New York City, the fourteenth major city visited in its nationwide investigation of organized crime.

It was clear from the testimony adduced before the Committee that there had been widespread commercially run gambling in Saratoga through August, the close of the racing season, in 1949. The state police did prevent the casinos from opening for the 1950 season. However, the record before the committee established, through the testimony of John A. Gaffney, Superintendent of State Police, that a report on gambling in Saratoga had been prepared at his request in 1947; that the report made it clear that gambling was going on full blast there; and, that when he received the report, Superintendent Gaffney simply filed the report in his own office. This seemed to indicate that the Superintendent of State Police was willfully avoiding his duty to forward the report to the Governor as well as his obligation to crack down on the gambling. It was also made clear, however, that historically, the mission of the State Police was to enforce the law in rural areas, not in cities; and, that the State Police would take the initiative in enforcing laws in cities only upon request of the city authorities or when ordered to do so by the Governor. It was also clear that someone who had risen to be Superintendent of State Police knew better than to forward to the Governor a report such as Superintendent Gaffney had commissioned in 1947, because no one could have suggested with a straight face that Governor Dewey did not know about the situation.[4]

Now, of course, everyone knew about the gambling in Saratoga. It had been going on as long as Saratoga had been a fashionable resort with horse racing as the centerpiece of its season. Anyone who spent any time in Saratoga knew of The Chicago Club, Delmonico's, Smith's Interlochen, Piping Rock, Arrowhead and Newman's Lake House, the city's most prominent gambling houses. And, of course, the committee's hearings in New York didn't tell the Governor anything he didn't already know, much as they would not have told any of his Democratic predecessors in office anything he didn't know-- which is probably why New York Democrats rarely did anything more than lightly jab the Governor about Saratoga. However, the fact that such notorious inhabitants of the underworld as Frank Costello, Joe Adonis and Meyer Lansky were partners in Saratoga's Piping Rock Casino as far back as 1933, when Senator Lehman was just beginning his first term as Governor, did not dim the spotlight on Governor Dewey's knowledge of the gambling in Saratoga and its criminal connections, which he must be presumed to have had at least as far back as his days as Special Prosecutor in the early 1930's, to say nothing of at least as far back as 1943, when he entered upon his first term as Governor. In short, the testimony about criminal activity, even though the activity itself was only gambling, when taken together with the apparent control of some of it by known criminals, suggested that perhaps the Governor, for purely political reasons, had been shutting his eyes to something in an upstate Republican bailiwick that was a little more serious than spitting on the sidewalk.

In addition to the matter of whether or not the Governor had been lax in connection with Saratoga, there was the attempt of the committee to seduce him into appearing as a witness. One did not have to be as astute a politician as Thomas E. Dewey to understand that the last thing in the world he should do would be to appear as a witness before the Kefauver Committee. As a result of his public exhibitions of criminal activities in Democrat-controlled big cities, Estes Kefauver had built up a significant amount of antagonism in the Democratic party,[5] a state of affairs hardly to be desired by a politician with Presidential aspirations. What better way to make himself more palatable to his own party than to splatter the most recent Republican nominee for President in front of a live television audience of millions of Americans,[6] to say nothing of all those who would witness this spectator sport on the evening news and read about it in the next morning's paper, and quite apart from all the cluck-clucking that would appear in editorials and political columns?

And so, the committee and the Governor played out their game. The Governor regretted that a virus prevented him from coming to New York, and hoped that the committee might be able to visit him in Albany. The *New York Times* reported that "Senator Kefauver . . . said that the committee has 'no intention' of going to Albany to get Governor Dewey's views on crime."[7]

The committee had created two political problems for the Governor. First, it had raised the issue of whether or not he had been diligent in the enforcement of the law in a Republican county. Second, it had raised the issue of whether the Governor was really interested in joining with the committee in the fight against crime--a slight hardly to be tolerated by one who had made his political career on his accomplishments as a prosecutor.

The first thing the Governor did was to have his own counsel look into the matter.[8] On March 28th, he followed this with the appointment of a Special Assistant Attorney General to conduct an investigation into the possible relationship, in Saratoga County, between gambling and those who ran it, and public officials and political figures.[9] The next thing the Governor did, one day later, was to create a State Crime Commission, constituted by five prominent people from different areas of public life, to investigate and take action against criminals and corrupt politicians. (Presumably to make clear his sense of urgency in the matter, the Governor notified former Appellate Division Justice Joseph M. Proskauer, his choice for Chairman of the Commission, of his appointment by radio-telephone to a ship near Gibralter on which he was taking a cruise.) The Governor's executive order also charged the Commission with the duty to determine whether there should be a new state agency to keep an eye on law enforcement.[10]

The State Crime Commission was a classic use of prominent citizens not identified with politics to defuse a dangerous political situation by taking it out of the partisan arena long enough so that everyone would forget the political situation which required its creation in the first place. It was not until the end of January, 1953 that the

Commission issued the first of its four reports, in which it recommended the establishment of a permanent Commission of Investigation.[11]

The Governor rejected the idea of a permanent crime commission. As a former prosecutor himself, he was not inclined to impose upon the state's district attorneys an executive superstructure, the utility of which was questionable, and the interference of which in the district attorneys' work was probable; and, therefore, he had no hesitancy in acceding to their opposition to it. Instead, he proposed the creation of the office of Commissioner of Investigation. The Commissioner would serve at the pleasure of the Governor, like any other cabinet officer, as a sort of personal, additional Attorney General, with the power to conduct investigations into state or local governmental irregularities at the direction of the Governor.[12] The enabling statute, the new section 11 of the State's Executive Law, became effective July 2, 1953. Its use as a political weapon awaited 1955.

Now, as far as the Republican county leaders, state legislators and all the other working politicians in the Party were concerned, to whom the implications and possible consequences of the Governor's proposal would have been apparent, the creation of this office was not received as a good idea, for the obvious reason that it would be an easily accessible and powerful political weapon in the hands of a Democratic Governor who wished to wage war against the Republican areas outside cities which predominated in the State, and which at the time of the agency's creation were increasing in electoral significance. Also, even though it was only in the short run, no Republican politician who was not personally and closely wedded to the Governor would have been interested in giving him more power to harass local organizations than he already had as undisputed boss of the Republican state organization.[13]

As for the Democrats, whether they did not want to seem to be against clean government or whether they figured that it might be a handy thing to have around if they struck it lucky in 1954, one can only speculate.

As for the Governor, it would appear that the Office of Commissioner of Investigation was simply an unintended consequence of his strategy for eliminating the Kefauver Committee Hearings as a source of embarrassment.

Notes

1. See William F. F. Young, *Thomas E. Dewey, et al.* (Denver, Outskirts Press, 2017): "Albany: Chapter 1 - Chapter 3".
2. In New York, the Supreme Court is the initial court of general juris-diction. The Appellate Division of the Supreme Court is the inter-mediate appellate court. New York's "Supreme Court" is its Court of Appeals.
3. Chapter 887, N.Y. Laws of 1953.
4. James A. Hagerty, "Senators Try To Tie Dewey to Gaming; Costello Balks Crime Inquiry Again; O'Dwyer Friend Challenged on Story," *New York Times*, March 17, 1951.
5. See William Howard Moore, "The Politics of Crime," chap. 6 in *The Kefauver Committee and the Politics of Crime 1950-1952* (University of Missouri Press, 1974).
6. According to a spokesman for the Consolidated Edison Company of New York, the use of an additional generator was required to sup-ply the necessry curent that was required during the public hear-ings in New York City. ("Extra Generator Needed For TV During Inquiry," *New York Times*, March 22, 1951.)
7. Warren Weaver, Jr., "Dewey Would Talk in Albany, But Senators Won't Go There," ibid., March 20, 1951.
8. See "Dewey Is Critical of Inquiry Actions," ibid., March 22, 1951; and ""Dewey Declines Comment," ibid., March 26, 1951.
9. "Dewey Sets Saratoga Inquiry And Plans State Crime Body," ibid., March 29, 1951.
10. "Dewey Names 5-Man Board To Investigate State Crime," ibid., March 30, 1951.
11. Warren Weaver, Jr., "State Crime Panel Urges 'Watchdog' To End Corruption,", ibid., January 26, 1953.
12. Warren Weaver, Jr., "Governor Rejects Crime "Watchdog" Sought By Inquiry," ibid., June 21, 1953.
13. Leo Egan, "Shapiro Inquiries Looking For Other G.O.P. Counties, ibid., February 13, 1956.

Chapter 3

W. Averell Harriman, the Democratic candidate, won the 1954 election for Governor. (He didn't win by much. To be precise, he won by 11,125 votes out of 5,110,351 cast, which is to say that he won by just over two tenths of one per cent of the vote.[1]) Then 62, Mr. Harriman had a record of continuous service as an appointed official in the domestic and foreign service of his country, beginning in 1933 under President Roosevelt, and ending with the administration of President Truman. He had started his public service after twenty years in the worlds of railroading, shipping and investment banking, which he had entered with the assistance of the seventy million dollar estate of his late father, E.H. Harriman, the Union Pacific Railroad magnate. There was never any question as to whether or why Mr. Harriman wanted to run for Governor in 1954. He wanted the Democratic nomination for President in 1956. He had been unsuccessful in his try for the nomination in 1952, when he and Estes Kefauver lost out to Adlai Stevenson. The most natural and effective thing to do to bolster his chances in 1956 would be to become Governor of the State of New York, an enviable asset for any aspirant for the Presidency.

The new Commissioner of Investigation was J. Irwin Shapiro. Mr. Shapiro had worked his way up the political ladder, starting in 1932 as an assistant district attorney in Queens County, following a short stint as a deputy assistant attorney general earlier that year. He had risen to Chief Assistant District Attorney by 1948, when he was named Acting District Attorney. In 1951, he gained the first rung of the judiciary in New York City when he was appointed a City Magistrate. Three years later, he went up a rung when he was appointed a Justice of the New York City Domestic Relations Court. When the Democrats gained the Governorship, he garnered the Queens County spot in the cabinet, Commissioner of Investigation.

On March 1, 1955, the new Commissioner of Investigation proudly announced that he had already begun seventy-one investigations. Mr. Shapiro's proclamation of his achievement occurred during a press conference, the primary purpose of which was to castigate the Republican controlled legislature for trimming the budget of the Office of the Commissioner of Investigation. He charged that we wanted to emasculate his office.[2] He was right. Of course, no one believed that Mr. Shapiro had actually started seventy-one investigations, since he didn't have any staff at that point. However, no one doubted for a moment that he had selected seventy-one Republican targets for investigation.

———— ◆ ————

On April 13, 1955, the Commissioner addressed the Brooklyn Bar Association.

It's always a good idea to see if you can arrange to be invited to speak to a bar association if you're a lawyer politician. It is not likely that the association will find you unqualified when your party nominates you for a judgeship, if you previously have been an invited guest speaker. If you're a public official, the invitation is easier to bring about than if you are not; and if you are a member of the Governor's cabinet, it is much easier. The availability of any reasonably prominent public person makes life easier for whoever is responsible for putting on a program, and it effects a patina of accomplishment for that person. When the speaker holds a statewide position of obvious importance, the appearance of the person also generates a feeling of gratitude on the part of the bar association as a whole, because the important public person has acknowledged the importance of the particular bar association. Also, if you're lucky, you may get some ink out of it. The Commissioner's remarks were set forth in a release from the Commissioner to the morning newspapers of April 14th.

Although a report of the event did not appear in the *New York Times*, the story may have been carried in other papers.

The title of the Commissioner's discourse was "State Commissioner of Investigation -- Gestapo or Public Watchdog?" He traced the historical differences between legislative and executive investigations, noted the procedural safeguards that New York State had in place for witnesses subpoenaed by the Commissioner, and made clear just how broad was the Commissioner's field for investigation. He gave a tip of the hat to "the investigator who has no desire to proceed other than in accordance with law and good morals" and articulated disapproval of the investigator "who would achieve his purposes at all costs." He concluded his remarks with the observation that the conduct of an investigation "depends essentially upon the character of the investigator."[3]

———•◆•———

Harry Brenner had been elected District Attorney of Suffolk County in 1952, after serving thirteen years as an assistant district attorney. In 1955, he was seeking his second three year term. His Democratic opponent, Henry Schantz, opening his campaign right after Labor Day at a Democratic rally in Southampton, charged that William S. Hart, the Republican Executive Assistant Director of Civil Defense for the county, was selling business supplies to Suffolk County departments. This, if true, was against the law. Henry warned that if Harry did not take action, he would take his evidence to the State Commissioner of Investigation.[4]

At the October 10th meeting of the Board of Supervisors, Milton L. Burns, the County Treasurer, presented a detailed report of the methodology of the sales of tax-delinquent properties, in response to Democratic campaign charges, circulated in the towns of Babylon and Brookhaven, of improprieties, if not illegalities in favor of well-connected Republicans.[5]

On October 27, 1955, Commissioner Shapiro announced that he had evidence that William S. Hart, who had resigned just a month earlier as executive assistant director of Suffolk County's Office of Civil Defense, had sold to the county some $17,000 worth of furniture--not an insubstantial amount of office furniture for county offices in those days--through undisclosed intermediaries while he was a county official. According to the Commissioner, what Hart had done was to arrange for a sale, and have another furniture dealer bill the county. The front would then pay Hart, after deducting a commission.[6] The reason Hart, a furniture dealer in his own right, had to go through a concealed middleman was that it was against the law for a county official to have private business dealing with the county. The Commissioner also made it known on October 27th that he had turned over his report on the investigation to Harry Brenner.[7]

———— ◆ ————

When the votes were counted, Harry Brenner was found to have led the ticket in the countywide races. On November 23rd, he announced that he had begun an investigation into the county's sale of tax properties.[8] On December 19th, following the grand jury's first session in which it addressed the subject of tax sales, it was disclosed that he had subpoenaed but had not yet received the personal financial records of John A. Britting, who was serving his first term as a member of the State Assembly from Suffolk County, following a twelve year tenure as Deputy County Treasurer. It was also disclosed that the grand jury would probably take up the matter of William S. Hart at its next session.[9]

On January 13, 1956, the *Times* reported that Commissioner Shapiro had charged that Assembyman Britting "had participated in 'fraudulent land deals' . . . which had cheated Suffolk County taxpayers out of millions of dollars in county-owned property" during his tenure as Deputy County Treasurer of Suffolk County from 1942 to 1955. The occasion for the Commissioner's statement to the press was the issuance of an order the Commissioner had obtained from the State Supreme Court in Manhattan, which directed John and his wife, Edna, to show cause on January 17th why they should not be found in contempt for their refusal, on January 5th, to answer questions about these transactions at the office of the Commissioner, located at 270 Broadway, the office building in lower Manhattan which housed the State of New York's New York City offices. (The Commissioner of Investigation had the statutory authority to subpoena and examine witnesses in his investigations.)[10]

————◆————

Prior to World War II, there had been no real activity in the buying and selling of land in the county for more than fifteen years, since, as was true across the country, there had not been very much residential or commercial construction following the onset of the Depression. During the war, there was money around to invest in land; but since one could not build during the war because of the unavailability of materials, and since one could not rationally predict when one would be able to build, there was no particular reason to buy vacant land. However, after the war, the shortage of housing, the availability of GI and FHA financing and the resultant birth of suburbia foreordained that the buying and selling and the improvement of real property would be, for decades to come, one of the county's biggest industries.

When the post-war building boom first started, there was a lot of suitable property available for purchase by tract builders. With the growth of suburbia, however, there were fewer and fewer individual tracts of a size which would enable a builder to build a lot of low-cost homes on them or, in the alternative, to create an enclave of high-priced homes--which would require a substantial land area for each home in order to command the higher price--large enough to make the whole thing worthwhile. Additionally, as time went on, the market value of unimproved property escalated as a function of the improvement of other property and the diminishing amount of vacant land.

The most common way of putting together a parcel of land large enough for a development was the one that would come first to anyone's mind, i.e., either to buy or purchase options to buy discrete connected parcels from their owners in the hope of ending up with a tract of substantial size. However, there was another way.

There were a lot of properties, amounting to thousands of lots on filed subdivision maps, most of which were situated in undeveloped, usually rather barren areas of the county, on which, even after the building boom was on, the real property taxes had not been paid, they not unreasonably having been viewed as being worth less than the taxes for which they were assessed. But, as we all know, beauty is in the eyes of the beholder, and there were beholders in the case of these properties on which the taxes had not been paid--speculators--who saw what is frequently not seen by those who live in an area, and what can be seen only by those who can have a more objective view because they are looking at things from a distance--to say nothing of into the distance. What these land dealers understood was that the push of residential development was increasing, and would continue to increase in an easterly direction. Consequently, what they saw was not land which, in its then present state, from the point of view of a prospective individual home buyer, was utterly un-prepossessing. What they saw were tremendous tracts of land which, in the hands of housing developers, would become entire, self-contained communities of people from the city whose idea of rural paradise would be houses surrounded by nothing but a lot of other houses--suburbia.

By the 1950's, there were hardly any tax-delinquent properties which by themselves were large enough to interest a tract builder. However, if one could combine a lot of moderately sized parcels of such land into a tract sizeable enough to be attractive to a developer, then one would have a highly marketable commodity to offer for sale. Moreover, such a sale would necessarily be an extremely profitable one, because notwithstanding statutory references to the "sale" of tax-delinquent property by a county and "bidding" at such a sale, one purchased tax delinquent property, subject to certain redemption rights on the part of the owner, by paying the county treasurer a fixed price constituted by the amount due for taxes, interest and expenses. The problem for one speculating in the tax-lien market was that on the day or days selected for the annual sale of a tax-delinquent properties, the county treasurer could accept the bid of anyone he chose; and there were a lot of people, including other speculators as well as many who were interested only in purchasing specific parcels for their own use, who would bid on these properties on tax sale day, which militated against one bidder achieving the desired agglomeration of a number of tax-delinquent parcels.

Now, as it happened, there was a time-honored practice of placing of holds on such property in Suffolk County; and the practice was quite legal under a 1940 resolution of the county's board of supervisors. If a hold was placed on a piece of such property, then one could come in at his convenience and pay whatever was due for taxes, interest and expenses. This was done for government, public service and eleemosynary purposes as well as for individuals. For example, in 1947, a hold had been put on a parcel of property for anticipated use by the New York National Guard. However, generally, holds were put on as accommodations for people for their private purposes. Since the county treasurer could accept a bid--which was really nothing more than a request to be allowed to pay the fixed price--from anyone he chose anyhow, on tax sale day, and since the price would be the same whether held for someone or sold on a tax sale day, the sale of a tax lien through a hold rather than on tax sale day was not consequential to the county, although obviously, it was consequential to the individual beneficiary of a hold, since he did not have to worry about whether he would be successful as a bidder on tax sale day.

However, whether for private or civic benefit, a hold would be put on a discrete tax-delinquent parcel; and except for the fact of political connection, in the case of an individual, or civic purpose, in the case of a governmental or civic recipient, there was no consideration for the courtesy. What our speculator friends did was to enter into an arrangement with the Deputy County Treasurer, John Britting, under which he would have holds placed on many individual parcels of delinquent properties which in the aggregate constituted sizeable tracts that were extremely attractive to developers. Having assembled a large enough parcel by means of the holds, a speculator could then enter into a contract of sale with a purchaser. He would then execute what was in effect his option to purchase the held properties for the usual fixed price, which, of course, was considerably less than the price at which he had contracted to sell them as a consolidated unit. The other difference between holds as a custom and the kind we are now talking about is that the speculators paid John Britting substantial sums of money for placing the holds on the properties they selected.

———— ◆ ————

From the report of the court proceedings on the Commissioner's application for the contempt citation, it appears that the Brittings had presented themselves at his office as required by their subpoena, but had asked for a two-week adjournment because of the illness of their attorney. The Commissioner refused, and was off on his quest for a contempt citation and a more public forum. When everybody appeared in court on January 17th, the Court arranged for dismissal of the contempt proceeding conditioned on the reappearance of the Brittings at the Commissioner's office, with counsel. Following the court session on the 17th, the Brittings' counsel noted the truth that the "holding" of property for prospective purchasers of property on which taxes had not been paid was a practice that had gone on for years. Counsel did not discuss whether taking money for rendering such a services was also a time-honored practice.[11]

The Britting matter quickly began to be referred to as the "Landgrab" scandal in *Newsday*, the daily newspaper servicing Nassau and Suffolk Counties. Overlooked in all the subsequent reports of the matter was the fact that the "millions of dollars" that the county's taxpayers were presumably cheated out of was a confection of the Commissioner's imagination. The reason it was a confection was not simply that the amount could not be calculated. It was a confection because the taxpayers could not be cheated out of any money, because they did not own the land to begin with. The taxpayers, through the county, held only tax liens on the properties. If Mr. Britting had not taken his bribes, the properties would not have brought any more money to the county than they did on the purchases by his silent partners.

The other striking example of the interesting use to which the Commissioner put words was in his description of the land sales as "fraudulent." In conjunction with the baseless charge that the sales to the speculators cheated the taxpayers out of money, it had the felicitous albeit subliminal effect of reinforcing the impression that somehow the taxpayers had been defrauded.

On February 1, 1956, Mr. Shapiro announced in the presence of Harry Brenner that he would be naming a special prosecutor to handle any case arising out of the Britting matter. Mr. Brenner stated that he had agreed to such a procedure because he knew all the people involved in the matter, he was a Republican, they were all

Republicans, and he did not want anyone to be able to accuse him or his staff of showing favor to any of the people involved as defendants or possible defendants.[12] Many raised their eyebrows when they read of this. After all, Harry had been conducting an investigation into the matter notwithstanding that the Brittings were Republicanss. Would he have asked for a special prosecutor if he had secured indictments?

On February 6th, John and Edna showed up at the Commissioner's office in accordance with the Court agreement, but took the Fifth Amendment.[13] On February 8, 1956, Assembly Speaker Ozzie Heck announced that the Assembly Committee on Ethics would take up the matter of Assemblyman Britting pleading the Fifth. If Britting had taken the Fifth in response to questions about his present position as an Assemblyman, he could have been removed for his action. However, the questions did not relate to any activity of his as an Assemblyman. The investigation would be the first under a Code of Ethics for legislators that had come into being in 1954. The Assembly had always possessed the power to expel any member it deemed unit for public office, although no one could remember whenever it had done so.

———— • ————

In a report dated February 10, 1956, the Commissioner submitted to the Governor the results of an investigation he had conducted of the county's purchasing practices.[14]

By the early 1950's, it had become apparent that Suffolk County's mixture of county and town government, which dated back to the time of Oliver Cromwell, was not up to the task of serving the increasing needs of the county's burgeoning population. The town supervisors, in addition to their township duties, administered the county's affairs as a collegiate body, its Board of Supervisors. Quite apart from this managerial nightmare, it was not possible under the existing governmental structure to furnish necessary county-wide services on a county-wide basis. This meant that the services could not be provided economically, and their cost could not be distributed equitably among the taxpayers. It was understood also that ultimately we would end up with a system similar to that which Nassau County, having had a significantly larger population than Suffolk before the Second World War, had been using since 1938. Essentially, it provided for provision of countywide services by the county, administered by its Board of Supervisors and a County Executive, with retention by townships and incorporated villages of their authority over local concerns. By the end of 1955, the Republican county leadership had determined upon its choice of the four alternatives offered by the State's Alternative County Government Law; and in January, 1956 a bill to accomplish the change would be introduced in the legislature.[15]

In May, 1953, however, before the effort to modernize the overall organization of the county's administration had gotten under way, the Board of Supervisors decided to take a step which signalized its belief that the county should start to move toward the goal of unified competitive purchasing for the county. The board's idea of the appropriate first step in this direction was to establish the office of Purchasing Agent, effective July 1st; and to appoint as Purchasing Agent the Clerk of the Board of Supervisors. However, although the board gave the title of Purchasing Agent to its Clerk, it did not bestow any staff (or additional remuneration for the responsibility of the office) upon the Clerk. In the meantime, by opting to have a purchasing agent, the county had put itself in a position of engaging in purchasing practices, some of which were not permitted for a county which had a purchasing agent, though they would have been perfectly legal had they not taken the first step, which was largely a symbolic one as far as they were concerned.

Essentially, the purchasing deficiency addressed by the report was that by 1955, when the Commissioner started looking for what he could focus on in Suffolk County, the move toward a modern purchasing operation, which comprehended not only competitive bidding but also wholesale purchasing, such as was employed by Nassau County, was still only a prospect. The report articulated two themes: First, the county was not as up to date as its neighbor. Secondly, by virtue of its establishment of the office of Purchasing agent in 1953 and then continuing to do business essentially as it had always done, its officials were only slightly less criminal than Al Capone.

The main part of the report consisted primarily of testimony of Republican officials, heavily larded with doses of sarcastic comments from the Commissioner. The highlight of the selected testimony that was included in the report was selections of the testimony of Raymond R. MacLean, the county's purchasing agent.

In 1936, Mr. MacLean had moved from New York City, where he had worked in a clerical capacity, to Bellport, in the town of Brookhaven. After some years as a bookkeeper in private business, he took the state civil service examination for Senior Account Clerk; and in 1943, he began his service with the county in that position. In August, 1954, he achieved the position of Clerk to the Board of Supervisors and that of Assistant Budget Director for the county, both of which were working, though non-civil service jobs, for which he was paid a total of less than $10,000. From the time of his appointment in 1954 to his testifying before the Commissioner of Investigation in 1955, he had conducted his activities as had his predecessor as Purchasing Agent, and as did the town officials and county departmental officials who had purchasing responsibilities, i.e., he bought from retail vendors whom the county had found to be satisfactory over the years.[16]

Heads of county departments who testified to similar practices, were rewarded in the report with freewheeling accusations of political favoritism. The Commissioner did not impute political chicanery to Mr. MacLean. However, in discussing Mr. Maclean's testimony, Mr. Shapiro opined that Mrs. MacLean would not buy a dozen eggs the way her husband bought county supplies; and in his Conclusions, the commissioner had no hesitancy in characterizing Mr. MacLean, who was the county's purchasing agent in name only, as an "uninitiative individual; entirely irresponsible and unfit." The Commissioner began the final portion of the report, denominated "Conclusions", as follows: "The method of purchasing followed in Suffolk County resulted in the following acts of criminal, quasi-criminal or unethical conduct:" The high point in the report was Mr. Shapiro's unqualified assertion that the entire Board of Supervisors, Mr. MacLean, Clarence Pulver, the County Auditor, and every county department head was guilty of criminal misfeasance. In the body of the report, the Commissioner, extrapolating from data which ranged in reliability from unsubstantiated to non-existent, had managed to confect wildly speculative figures for savings the county had lost by not having a purchasing system such as Nassau's; and, of course, in his summary, the Com-

missioner referred to his lost-savings figures as indisputably established.

The report ended with the following peroration:

> This is the first of three reports that I intend to make
> to Your Excellency dealing with Suffolk County. With
> the submission of the last report, I shall recommend
> the adoption of certain steps, to make certain that all
> criminal wrongdoing committed by various public of-
> ficials of Suffolk County shall not go unpunished.

A summary of the report and a reproduction of its Conclusions
and Recommendations were presented by the *Times* on February
13th.[17] As it happened, although the report had been issued to the
Governor and presented to the press, it had not been sent to the
board of supervisors, or anyone else referred to in the report. And so,
that evening, following a five-hour meeting of seven of the eight Republican members of the Board of Supervisors, R. Ford Hughes, the
Republican County Leader, and others forming the Republican leadership in the county, Philipp A. Hattemer, Chairman of the Board of Supervisors, wired the Governor asking for copies of the report.
(According to us, the first we knew about the report were the newspaper stories about it. This was somewhat disingenuous. As the *Times*
put it so delicately, "[t]he official Republican position . . . was that it
was 'only through the newspapers' that county officials knew anything
of [Mr. Shapiro's charges]."[18]) However, the Commissioner's lapse of
etiquette gave us a basis for going on a counteroffensive with some
degree of safety. The Commissioner complied with the request.[19]

On February 16th, the two Democratic members of the board,
as well as the six Republican members present and voting, adopted a
resolution which charged the Commissioner of Investigation with deliberately abusing "decent standards of fairness" in the way he conducted the investigation, referring in particular to the fact that just
about everyone accused of misfeasance had not been given an opportunity to testify, and in the way in which he reached his conclusions and wrote his report.[20] A couple of weeks later, the back and

forth about the report would begin again when a report on Suffolk County operations was released by the state's Department of Audit and Control.[21]

———————— ✦ ————————

When the Commissioner's first report was issued, just one week previously, Ford Hughes, after noting that it was "exactly what we expected of Mr. Shapiro," described the Commissioner's activity as "a one-sided political investigation."[22] The comment was fair enough. The same day, the *Times* carried the story about the report on county purchasing methods, it also published an article by Leo Egan, one of its leading political columnists, from which it was evident that everyone in politics understood that Commissioner Shapiro was simply the point man in the Democrats' effort to cut into Republican strength in suburban and upstate counties by a campaign designed to induce the voters to throw the Republican rascals out; and, that Suffolk county was the first major trial run for that strategy.[23] Moreover, it was only right that Ford Hughes go on record to say, as he did, "We still feel that our public officials have a great deal of integrity."[24] After all, with the exception of the report's reference to William H. Hart, who sold furniture to the county while on the county payroll (and who, as events would show, did conspire to hide the fact), the report was essentially a reckless shotgun showering of charges of criminality against the officials, only a few of which were even attempted to be proven, and none of which ever were or could have been sustained.

The problem for us was, as it always is when one is defending against a political offensive that is presented to the public as an inquiry into the integrity and caliber of governance, that the result of the inquiry had been settled upon before the first disclosure of a discovery of inefficiency or wrongdoing. What the lay citizen perceives as the natural consequence of a growing disgust on the part of the electorate at an initially distasteful, then annoying, then quite unacceptable, and finally really insupportable state of corruption or lack of ability on the part of a party in power in a political unit to administer governmental affairs or police itself, usually turns out, upon any disinterested retrospective analysis, to have been the result of carefully orchestrated manipulation of the voters. The out-group knows this perfectly well, but of course keeps it to itself, since it is doing the composing as well as the orchestrating. The in-group knows it perfectly well, but it never does it any good to articulate this truth in public, because every party in power, whether it be in the smallest village, the largest township in a county or the county itself, or if it be on those macro-political levels--the ones we read about in the instant-history political columns in newspapers and magazines that seem to have been with us always and which now appear also as scripts on television news shows--the city, state and federal governments--whether it's them or us, the outfit in power is always going to have the irreducible minimum of bumblers, thieves and people whose tongues come out with just the right things for the other side to hop on. If you're in power, there's always going to be something you're doing wrong, and there's always going to be someone who's doing wrong. And so, if you say that it isn't necessarily so that where there's smoke there's fire, and that the smoke people think they see and smell is simply a smoke screen being put up by the people out of power just so they can get into office, sure as shooting someone is going to announce the discovery of a fire--a fire, by the way, that everybody on both sides always knew was burning.

On February 17th, the Commissioner issued his second report to the Governor, entitled, "REPORT OF INVESTIGATION OF THE ENFORCEMENT OF THE VEHICLE AND TRAFFIC LAWS OF THE STATE IN SUFFOLK COUNTY".[25]

The Commissioner explained in the second paragraph of his sixty-four page report that the investigation "was dictated by the great public interest and alarm over the rising automobile rate everywhere in the nation and by the fact that such an inquiry would provide a test of the quality and effectiveness of the administration of justice in the lower courts of Suffolk County." He observed that although Suffolk County had only 1.9% of the state's population, it had 2.6% of the state's accidents. He then went on to suggest that "[a] contributory cause for this tragically high accident rate may well be the general breakdown of the enforcement of the vehicle and traffic laws by the courts of Suffolk County."[26]

It is true that the Commissioner's comparison of the county's percentage of the state's population with the county's percentage of the state's motor vehicle accidents was based upon census figures for 1950 and accident figures for 1954, during a period of spectacular population growth relative to almost all the other counties in the state as well as in absolute terms. It is also true that to say that there was a "general breakdown of the enforcement of the vehicle and traffic laws by the courts of Suffolk County" was somewhat hyperbolic. Nonetheless, the report, which was referable to the disposition of motor vehicle infractions by the Justices of the Peace in the Town of Islip, disclosed through admissions by some justices of the peace themselves, that in response to requests from such people as a chief of police, other justices of the peace, the Chief Investigator of the District Attorney's office, and assorted Republican politicians, they had given suspended sentences in speeding cases, and not entered records of convictions on the backs of the defendants' drivers' licenses. The net result was that in these cases, the state's motor vehicle bureau, which was in the early stages of implementing a system for the suspension and revocation of drivers' license that was based upon both numbers and types of moving motor vehicle infractions, was without knowledge of the convictions.

The sampling of cases was not random. Also, it was rather obvious that in the time frame in which the Commissioner was operating, he simply scooped up as many cases as he could find in which the favors were granted. Moreover, the number of cases in which these courtesies were granted formed an insignificant percentage of the total of moving violation cases before the town's justices of the peace. Nonetheless, it was clear that the requests for favorable consideration were granted as a matter of course. Moreover, we even transmitted our requests in writing, and our friends at court did not even bother to remove them from the files. The *Times*, in addition to its story about the report, which included some of the choicer factual tidbits, some of the Commissioner's particularly florid comments, and a presentation of the Commissioner's conclusions and recommendations, featured a picture of a typewritten letter on official stationery from Sheriff McCollum to Moses Drake, one of the Justices of the Peace. The letter began, "Dear Mose", and went on to say that "a good friend of our organization" (whose name had appeared twice in the letter but subsequently had been erased by Justice Drake before disposing of the matter) had written to the Sheriff inquiring if anything could be done to help the recipient of the enclosed speeding ticket.[27]

On one hand, you had to hand it to the Commissioner or whoever had the inspiration to do an investigation, the subject matter of which was fixing traffic tickets. Moreover, the sixty-four page report itself was a masterful combination of selected testimony and the Commissioner's political invective, the latter offered in the report and appearing in the newspaper stories as his relation of the facts. On the other hand, without detracting from the Commissioner's performance as a sarcastic, overbearing examiner of sitting-duck witnesses (after all, the JP's did honor a fair number of requests for leniency, both within and without the law) or as a polemicist, you could not say in truth that we didn't extend every possible assistance to him. After all, it was beyond belief that any self-respecting Democratic District Leader in New York City would have made a written memorandum of a request for fixing a ticket, or that any New York City Democratic Magistrate, regardless of his inadequacy for the bench, would have been so brainless as to make written reference to such political chores in court records.

The report constituted the second institutional move by the Commissioner in the process of creating a setting in which the establishment by the Governor of an Extraordinary Special and Trial Term of the Supreme Court for Suffolk County to conduct a continuing inquiry could be presented as not only appropriate but necessary for the proper execution of the responsibilities of the office of Governor. Predictably, therefore, the second report's concluding paragraph was remarkably similar to that of the first report:

> This is the second of three reports that I intend to make to Your Excellency dealing with Suffolk County. As stated in the first report, dated Feb. 10, 1956, I shall, with the submission of the final report, make certain recommendations directed toward insuring that the criminal acts committed by various Suffolk County public officials shall not go unpunished.[28]

The Republican County Leader could, as he did, whine the truth for the newspapers, i.e., that "the present investigation is politically inspired and is being carried out for the sole purpose of discrediting the Republican Party in Suffolk County." Charlie Maier, the Superintendent of Highways and Republican town leader of Islip, could, as he did, ask why the report made no mention of the fact, conveyed to the Commissioner, that Adrian Mason, the Democratic County Leader of Suffolk County who had become a Deputy Commissioner of the State Department of Motor Vehicles on Mr. Harriman's accession to the governorship, had interceded on at least four occasions for Islip residents. Mr. Maier could, as he also did with justification, point out that the Commissioner   used such words as "fixer", "fix" and "contract" in the report without factual foundation.[29] All of this was true and was fair comment. The problem was that these were the only things we could say. The one thing we would have liked to have been able to say--that the whole thing was a fabrication--we could not do. And we certainly couldn't take a chance on saying that the JP's--and also the people who interceded with them--were much misunderstood. Once the three-headed horse is out of the stable, it's very difficult to persuade people who have seen it ambling around town that it doesn't exist. And while the question, "Well, what's so strange about a three-headed horse?", might be regarded as whimsy, the question, "Well, what's such a big deal about fixing some traffic tickets?" is not likely to be regarded so kindly by most voters, since most voters are unable to have their traffic tickets fixed. All one can do by way of a public response is to come as close to the line as possible to suggesting, without actually doing so, that the asserted wrongdoing is not important in itself as an affront to basic human values. The Presiding Justice of the Appellate Division of the Second Department, which embraces Suffolk County, was obviously affronted however. The day after the report appeared in the newspapers, he requested the Commissioner to file charges, because although the Appellate Division had the authority to remove the justices of the peace, it could not, on its own motion, institute a removal proceeding.[30]

———— ◆ ————

By this time, sufficient groundwork had been laid for the convening of an Extraordinary Special and Trial Term of the Supreme Court, which would enable our friends on the other side to flay us in public for an indeterminate period of time. There was not only the Commissioner's first report, which asserted criminality in the context of large sums of public monies squandered, followed a week later by the second report, which, despite its flamboyant misrepresentations, contained evidence from the mouths of justices of the peace which surely would result in their removal from office by the Appellate Division of the Supreme Court, but also the Commissioner's statements for the press one month previously about John Britting, an ingenious blending of a justified charge against Britting (he took bribes) with a fantasized assertion of loss to the taxpayers (that they had been cheated out of millions of dollars) and the false suggestion that other public officials (not then or ever named) had been involved in Britting's illegal conduct (they had "concurred" in the transactions).

Thus, it was no surprise that on February 27th, the *Times* advised that the Governor would be taking the next step as soon as an agreement was reached on the selection of a special prosecutor. The Attorney General could appoint a special assistant attorney general to handle such a matter, but only upon the request of the Governor. However, the Attorney General was Jacob K. Javits, the only Republican to win statewide office in the 1954 election; and obviously, the Governor would not make such a request of the Republican Attorney General in the absence of an accord on the matter. Alternatively, the convening of an extraordinary grand jury could go ahead if the District Attorney of Suffolk County appointed a special assistant district attorney who was acceptable to the Governor.

The *Times* further reported that the Commissioner had advised that he and Attorney General Javits were "confident" that they shortly would be able to reach an agreement on the procedure for selecting a prosecutor; and, upon the selection itself; and that the Commissioner also announced that his third report, dealing with the sales of tax liens would be submitted to the Governor around the middle of March. On this occasion, he referred to the forthcoming report as the "land grabs" report.[31] Thereafter, more often than not, newspaper stories about John Britting and the sales of tax liens referred to the "land grabs report"--and eventually, to the "land grabs" indictments, the "land grabs" trial, the "land grabs" verdict, the sentences in the "land grabs" case, and the ruling on appeal and other legal matters related to the "land grabs" case. Again, the Commissioner had come up with a felicitous phrase, for it surely suggested the wrongful taking of land from the taxpayers (as distinguished from the aggressive taking away from other speculators the opportunity to purchase the tax liens in question--for which they would have been delighted, of course, to pay as much money as John Britting's clients paid to him).

On February 28th, by way of an unintentional publicity assist to our friends on the other side, John Britting announced that he would not be seeking renomination as an Assemblyman in the spring primary election. The announcement contained a comment on the inquiry into tax sale matters by the Commissioner of Investigation, which began, "I have never consciously committed any wrongful act . . .", which was about the only thing he could safely say about himself in the circumstances, and which he ended by somewhat gratuitously associating himself with other public officials who had been referred to by the Commissioner: "I ask the good and fair-minded people of my county not to pre-judge [sic] me or any other officer of the county presently under attack. I am confident that, given a chance, these officers will be completely exonerated."[32] More than one on our side wondered how the county leader came to allow this to happen, for, as the *Times* noted, "Mr. Britting's withdrawal from public life was announced through the office of R. Ford Hughes, Republican County chairman. Mr. Hughes declined to comment on the statement."[33]

On March 1st, the Department of Audit and Control issued its biennial report for the county. It contained the normal nitpicking of state auditors with respect to items that have no governmental significance (e.g., the District Attorney's office forgot to turn over to the County Treasurer $324 confiscated in bookmaker raids until reminded to do so following an audit of its books). It also contained references to matters which did represent violations of law, though they did not bring to mind moral turpitude. For example, the sheriff, one of the county's supervisors and the county clerk each held a directorship in a bank which held county deposits; and the county's two coroners had accepted witness fees in criminal cases. It noted that the County auditor's examinations of the county's various departments and institutions were not conducted annually, as required by law. It urged the creation of a Department of Purchases, the next logical step after establishing the office of Purchasing Agent. It took the position that in many situations where such action was required under the law, the Purchasing Agent had failed to advertise for bids; and, that the Purchasing Agent had rejected low bids on two occasions without explanation.[34]

None of the foregoing was unusual; and in any event, the mission of the Department of Audit and Control was to audit the state's political subdivisions for compliance with all matters within its jurisdiction. It was required to recite a noncompliance which was an inadvertence of no consequence just as it was obliged to report a gross violation that would shock the conscience of the community. Moreover, it was bound to make a determination of compliance or noncompliance on a matter such as advertising for bids on the basis of its interpretation of the law. However, the report also declared as fact that the Republican county leader had shared illegally in the purchase of county-owned land; and, that Edna Britting, the wife of Assemblyman John Britting, had bought county land illegally while her husband had been Deputy County Treasurer. It noted the fact that the sheriff's son had purchased land from the county and thereafter transferred title to his father. It also stated the fact that William S. Hart, while Assistant Director of Civil Defense, had sold office furniture to the county; and, that George W. Still, while Public Administrator of the county, had purchased insurance policies from the insurance firm of which he was a partner.[35]

———— ♦ ————

In between the issuance of the Controller's report and our rebuttal, we learned that the eminent epistler, Hon. William C. McCollum, Sheriff of Suffolk County, had declared that he would not be seeking re-election, taking care to make it clear that his decision to retire from public life was in no way connected with the recent publicity accorded him in both of the Commissioner of Investigation's reports. The Sheriff said that he had told Ford Hughes more than a year previously that his present term would be his last. As he put it, "I think twenty years in office is enough." On one hand, this could have been the truth, since the Sheriff was then seventy-four years old.[36] On the other hand, being Sheriff was neither like digging ditches nor like plotting the paths of stars. His age, barring the onset of serious physical infirmity or senility, would not have been an impediment to the continued execution of his office, which was essentially a political sinecure, bearing no relation to the office of sheriff in *The Lone Ranger*. (Leonard W. Hall had held the same position in Nassau County before he went on to the Congress and the chairmanship of the National Republican Committee.) It was too bad in a way. Bill McCollum's beefsteak dinners, which he put on at county headquarters during the summer months, were deservedly famous. Everybody liked Bill McCollum, including a lot of our friends on the other side, who were hopeful that the beefsteak affairs would continue.

———————•◆•———————

The day after Beefsteak Bill's announcement of his retirement, Phil Hattemer, our chairman of the Board of Supervisors, charged that the report of Audit and Control was political.[37] Three weeks later, following the issuance of the Commissioner's second report to the Governor, the Democratic State Controller, Arthur Levitt, demurred.[38] Then, the entire Board of Supervisors took the position that the Controller had explicitly approved the purchasing procedures which Audit and control had criticized in its report and which Commissioner shapiro had condemned in his report (All of them, not just the Republican members, had been accused of criminal misfeasance).[39] Then the Controller issued a statement saying that he had been misunderstood.[40]

Standard stuff. The possibility that the Audit and Control report would not have been as supportive of the Commissioner of Investigation's report wherever and to the greatest extent it could be never existed. Moreover, Governor Dewey's legislation which established the office of Commissioner of Investigation directed that the Commissioner receive from every state department any assistance and cooperation that he might request in the performance of his duties. Thus, it was not only natural but quite legal for the Commissioner and the Controller to work as a team. It was also quite obvious, from the assertions of illegality referable to land transactions of Ford Hughes and Edna Britting, and from the statement about Sheriff McCollum, that the Controller had, in fact, worked hand in glove with the Commissioner.

———————◆———————

As things turned out, no agreement between Messrs. Shapiro and Javits had to be reached. The way was cleared for the Governor to have who he wanted as special prosecutor in an unexpected fashion. On March 14th, he disclosed that Harry Brenner, our Republican District Attorney, had resigned, effective March 20th.[41]

No one ever explained to anyone else's complete satisfaction just why Harry Brenner resigned. There were a number of theories, all of which were plausible. When the press questioned Ford Hughes about it, he implied that he had suggested to him that he resign. He said that he had talked to him before the resignation, and he also said that "in view of all the allegations," (whatever that was supposed to encompass), he thought that he "was not the man who should act as prosecutor."[42] This explanation was the least credible of all those that were considered, since it was never contemplated by anyone that Harry, himself, would be the prosecutor. For the same reason, the grace note of Mr. Hughes' comments to the press, "Having leveled these charges, the Democrats should be put in the position of proving them,"[43] was equally devoid of logic.

Harry Brenner himself gave two reasons for his action. The first, patently disingenuous, was that by resigning, he would enable the county to avoid having to pay for two prosecutors and staffs; and the second, not at all unlikely, that he would thereby put an end to insinuations about his integrity as district attorney that went back to his 1955 reelection campaign.[44]

Henry Schantz, Harry's Democratic opponent when he ran for his second term in 1955, had made no bones about the fact that someone must be sitting on what he plainly enough indicated was hanky panky in connection with the dispostion of tax lien properties. And so, while no one ever suggested or believed that Harry was *particeps criminalis* with Britting, or in any other way involved in anything improper, there were those who did make a connection between Henry Schantz's references to official inaction on what he had referred to as the tax lien situation during the 1955 campaign, Commissioner Shapiro's reference to other public officials having "concurred" in Britting's activities, and what Harry, in his resignation statement, referred to as his "more personal reason for resigning."

In any event, the resignation made things simple enough for the Governor. All he had to do was appoint as District Attorney of Suffolk County whomever the Democratic organization was going to run in November for a full term. It turned out to be George W. Percy, Jr., a former Assistant United States Attorney.

And so, when the Governor averred at the press conference called to announce Mr. Percy's appointment on March 16th, that it was a "non-political appointment," and that he had not consulted with the Democratic county organization on the selection--adding that ordinarily, he would have done so, but that "in this case, I want this absolutely clean out of politics",[45] butter wouldn't have melted in Ford Hughes' mouth. It certainly wasn't that he was as credulous as the *Times* writer who stated as fact that George "had not had the customary clearance with the Suffolk Democratic organization".[46] More likely, it was just that he thought he might as well take the opportunity to appear as squeaky clean as the Governor. He therefore volunteered all possible assistance to the new district attorney from Republican county officials, called for the punishment of the guilty and the exoneration of the innocent, and praised George as "an outstanding lawyer and member of a long-distinguished county family."[47]

Notes

1. "Harriman Margin Lowest Since 1850," *New York Times*, December 17, 1954.
2. Leo Egan, "G.O.P. Set to Cut Budget To Rule Out State Tax Rise," ibid., March 1, 1955.
3. "FROM: JUDGE J. IRWIN SHAPIRO, Commissioner of Investigation of the State of New York": "RELEASE TO MORNING NEWSPAPERS OF THURSDAY, APRIL 14, 1955" (New York State Library, Government Documents)
4. "Schantz Says CD official Sells Supplies to County," *Long Islander*, September 8, 1955.

The *Long Islander*, for the entire period covered by this work, was a broadsheet that was the primary weekly newspaper for the township of Huntington.

5. "County Treasurer Refutes Charges on Tax Land Sales," ibid., October 13, 1955.
6. "Suffolk Ex-official Is Linked to Fraud," *New York Times*, October 28, 1955.
7. Ibid.
8. "Brenner Announces Investigation of Sales Tax Land," *New York Times*, November 24, 1955.
9. "Burns Only Witness as Brenner Opens Tax Sale Inquiry," *Long Islander*, December 22, 1955.
10. "Britting Accused in Suffolk Fraud," *New York Times*, January 13, 1956.

There does not appear to be any reference to this matter in either the *New York Times* or the *Long Islander* between December 22, 1955 and January 13, 1956.

11. "Suffolk Official to Face Inquiry," ibid., January 18, 1956.
12. "Aide to be Named in Suffolk Inquiry," ibid., February 1, 1956.
13. "Legislator Invokes Fifth Amendment," ibid., February 7, 1956.
14. J. Irwin Shapiro, Commissioner of Investigation, *Report of Investigation of Methods of Purchasng in Suffolk County*, (Trials: Ind. 2418, Law Library, New York State Library, Albany).
15. "County Executive System Is Proposed for Suffolk," *New York Times*, January 5, 1956.
16. "Purchasing Chief Vague About Job," ibid., February 13, 1956.
17. Clayton Knowles, "Illegal Spending by Suffolk Aides Charged by State," and "Suffolk Inquiry Findings," ibid., February 13, 1956.
18. Clayton Knowles, "Suffolk Republicans Ask to See Charges," ibid., February 14, 1956.
19. "Report on Suffolk Mailed by Shapiro," ibid., February 15, 1956.
20. Clayton Knowles, "Officials in Suffolk Call Inquiry Unfair And Deny Illegality," ibid., February 17, 1956.
21. "Audit in Suffolk Shows Misdeeds State Declares," ibid., March 2, 1956.
22. "Hughes Decries Report As One-Sided Finding," ibid., February 13, 1956.

23. Leo Egan, "Shapiro Inquiries Looming For Other G.O.P. Counties," ibid.
24. "Hughes Decries Report as One-Sided Finding," ibid.
25. Trials Indiv. No. 2417, Law Library, New York State Library, Albany.
26. Ibid.
27. Clayton Knowles, "Shapiro Accuses Suffolk Judges Of Ticket Fixing," *New York Times*, February 20, 1956.
28. Trials Indiv. No. 2417, Law Library, New York State Library, Albany.
29. "G.O.P. In Suffolk Rebukes Shapiro," *New York Times*, February 22, 1956.
30. "Suffolk Judges Facing Removal," ibid., February 21, 1956.
31. "Harriman to Act on Suffolk Soon," ibid., February 27, 1956
32. "Britting Not to Run in Suffolk Primary," ibid., February 29, 1956.
33. Ibid.
34. "Audit in Suffolk Shows Misdeeds, State Declares," *New York Times*, March 2, 1956.
35. Ibid.
36. "Suffolk Sheriff Going," *New York Times*, March 3, 1956.
37. "Suffolk Report Scored," ibid., March 5, 1956.
38. "Suffolk Charges Denied by Levitt," ibid., March 26, 1956.
39. "Suffolk's Board Upheld by Levitt," ibid., March 27, 1956.
40. "Levitt Clarifies Suffolk Letter," ibid., March 28, 1956.
41. "Brenner Resigns Office in Suffolk," ibid., March 15, 1956.
42. Ibid.
43. Ibid.
44. "Brenner Gives Resignation to Governor; Democrats to Prosecute Own Charges," *Long Islander*, March 15, 1956.
45. "Governor Names G. W. Percy Jr. To Be Suffolk District Attorney," *New York Times*, March 17, 1956.
46. "D. A. For Suffolk," ibid., March 18, 1956.
47. "Hughes Promises to Aid," ibid., March 17, 1956.

Chapter 4

On March 23rd, the Suffolk County Democratic organization duly designated George W. Percy, Jr. to be its nominee for District Attorney in the fall election.[1]

On March 29th, the Governor's office announced that it had received Commissioner Shapiro's "land grabs" report; that the report had been transmitted to District Attorney Percy "for appropriate action"; that the report disclosed the involvement of previously unnamed Suffolk County officials; and, that the report would not be made public. Commissioner Shapiro explained that to make it public "might impair prosecutions."[2] No other official was ever publicly named. The report was never released.

On April 11th, the Commissioner filed formal charges against Islip Justice of the Peace Drake, Justice of the Peace Rudolph Kammerer of Southold, and Justice of the Peace Clarence Duffield of Brookhaven, and petitioned the Appellate Division to remove them from office.[3]

On April 25th, our new district attorney formally requested the Governor to appoint an Extraordinary Special and Trial Term of the Supreme Court for Suffolk County.[4]

On May 3rd, Commissioner Shapiro filed formal charges against two additional justices of the peace: Charles F. Pfeifle, of Babylon, and Lester H. Davis of Brookhaven.[5]

On May 4th, the Governor ordered the convening of an Extraordinary Trial and Special term of the Supreme Court. By the terms of the Governor's order, the extraordinary term was to last "as long as it may be necessary," and its subject matter comprehended not only "unlawful acts involving public money or property, public records, voting, tax collections, influencing of public officers, corporations employing former public officers [and] those who do business with the county and local government," but additionally, "anyone who might attempt to hinder the investigation itself."[6]

As part of its story about the Governor's action, the *New York Times* summarized the three reports on Suffolk County which had been submitted by Commissioner Shapiro to the Governor. Recalling that the third report had not been made public, but instead had been sent directly to George Percy, it commented, "The lack of publicity on the third report was attributed to Mr. Harriman's growing conviction that the first two had not been sufficiently dispassionate and impartial for the type of serious indictment they constituted."[7]

On May 10th, Commissioner Shapiro obtained an order directing Martin J. Stein, a real estate operator from Great Neck, in Nassau County, to show cause why he should not be held in contempt for refusing to answer questions about a Britting tax lien deal in which Mr. Britting had been the silent partner of Mr. Stein. In the affidavit in support of his request for the order to show cause, the Commissioner asserted that on the same day Mr. Stein redeemed tax delinquent property for $54,800, he did two other things: He sold it for $281,000, and gave John and Edna Britting a check for $56,550. The Commissioner could not resist adding that "without one penny of investment, the Brittings on this single deal profited to the extent of $56,550."[8]

The next day, the Extraordinary Special and Trial Term was convened by Supreme Court Justice George Tilzer, whom the Governor had reassigned from his normal duties in Bronx County to handle the Suffolk County chore.[9]

On May 20th, Commissioner Shapiro obtained an order directing Albert G. Glass, a real estate operator from Lindenhurst, in the town of Babylon, to show cause why Mr. Glass, whom the Commissioner characterized as "Suffolk County's biggest land speculator," should not be held in contempt for refusing to answer questions about a Britting tax lien deal in which Mr. Britting had been the silent partner of Mr. Glass. In the affidavit in support of his request for the order to show cause, the Commissioner stated in substance that by a combination of himself, his mother and a corporate dummy, Mr. Glass redeemed tax delinquent property for $93,920, sold it for $465,300, and gave John Britting not less than $14,530. The Commissioner noted that the contract of sale to the ultimate purchaser, a builder, was entered into on October 14, 1954, three weeks before the tax delinquent property was redeemed by Mr. Glass. Again, the Commissioner could not resist adding that Mr. Britting profited from the transaction "without investing one red cent." While the reference to "one red cent" was not necessary in order for the Commissioner to obtain his order to show cause, a little inflammatory icing for the newspapers is hardly something to get excited about in a scandals investigation. However, under the safety of his affidavit in a court proceeding, the Commissioner took the occasion to rebroadcast the fantasy about Mr. Britting's covert business activities costing the taxpayers money. Mr. Shapiro stated, "It is obvious that a legitimate sale, properly conducted, would have brought this profit of about $370,000 into the County Treasurer's hands, instead of going into the pockets of a private land grabber."[10] The fanfare about losses of money to the taxpayers (whose real property taxes were skyrocketing from significant rises in school taxes) as a result of John Britting's operations was much more to be feared by us than the fact of John Britting taking bribes. Yet one could not publicly take the position that the bribes didn't cost the taxpayers anything, because then one would be implying that there really wasn't anything so bad about John having been on the take. The Commissioner, or whoever was doing his thinking for him, was one smart apple.

———— ♦ ————

On June 1st, the Appellate Division appointed Frank F. Adel, a retired Justice of the Appellate Division, as referee to conduct the removal proceeding that had been instituted against the justices of the peace; and it designated Commissioner Shapiro as the prosecutor in the proceeding.[11] On June 18th, the hearing began. The testimony adduced by the Commissioner made a pretty good case against the seventy-five year old Moses Drake, mostly out of the mouth of the venerable JP, for acceding to requests for leniency for traffic violators from a wide range of citizens. Justice Drake quite candidly acknowledged that he had received requests from Ford Hughes on behalf of traffic violators, and even one which he understood to be from Johnny Crews, the Republican leader of Kings County. The Commissioner, no tyro in the courtroom, easily got Mr. Drake to concede that he couldn't remember an instance of not giving favorable consideration to a request by Mr. Hughes.[12]

Mr. Crews subsequently came to the hearing, acknowledged he knew the defendant in the case referred to by Justice Drake, and then uttered a somewhat less than categorical denial of intervention: "I never spoke to Judge Drake about anything."[13] Mr. Hughes was more direct when he took the stand. He acknowledged that while he had never personally intervened with Justice Drake, such calls were made from party headquarters in his name. Also refreshing for his candor was A. Russell Richards, the chief investigator for the District Attorney's office, who had been mentioned in Commissioner Shapiro's report. (Although none of Russ Richards' communications made the *Times*, the ticket-fixing report itself contained a photocopy of one of his communications, which sought leniency for a person who had acted faithfully as an informer.) Admitting intervention with JP's other than Justice Drake, Richards, who had been a civil service investigator since 1934, and Chief Investigator since 1949, characterized such efforts as being "almost an occupational hazard in the prosecutor's office."[14]

Moses Drake was represented by Guy O. Walser, by then for some years the senior partner of the old line firm of Robbins, Wells and Walser. Mr. Walser was courtly, extremely capable as a trial and appellate lawyer, and highly regarded at the bar. He presented several character witnesses on behalf of Judge Drake. One of the witnesses testified that Judge Drake's reputation for integrity was "wonderful." On cross-examination, the Commissioner asked him whether he would say the same thing if it were shown that Judge Drake had accepted gratuities. The answer was "Yes." While Judge Drake and Mr. Walser no doubt were pleased with the reply, the answer was not as important as the question, which only served to confirm to Mr. Walser that if he examined Judge Drake as his own witness, the Commissioner, who had the right to impeach the Judge's credibility as a witness on behalf of himself, would ask the Judge questions about gratuities, and might even offer evidence on the subject. Therefore, although Mr. Walser had previously indicated that he would call Judge Drake as a witness, he rested his case without doing so, thus depriving the Commissioner of having some fun with the old gentleman. The Commissioner was nettled, because he now had to explain to the referee why he had made reference to gratuities without any evidence having been offered about gratuities. His explanation was that he expected Judge Drake to take the stand in his own behalf, and that he knew that on his cross-examination of Judge Drake he could establish the Judge's acceptance of gratuities. Of course, Mr. Walser could have objected to the Commissioner's question to the character witness, but he was not just out of law school, and preferred to look forward to see Mr. Shapiro swing slowly in the air as he made his obligatory excuses to the referee.[15]

The other JP's were represented by W. Royden Klein, of Smithtown. On June 25th, Mr. Klein stipulated into the record the testimony of forty witnesses taken by the commissioner about Southampton Town Justice of the Peace Rudolph Kammerer (it had not been included in the ticket-fixing report, which focused only on Islip JP's), and called neither Judge Kammerer nor any other witness on his behalf, although he indicated that he would be submitting three character endorsements by letter. Mr. Klein's defense for Judge Kammerer and the other four JP's he was representing was simply that none of the Commissioner's evidence constituted wrongdoing.

The testimony showed that Judge Kammerer played no favorites as between Republican and Democratic politicians; and, that he was as likely to respond favorably to requests from gas station attendants, bartenders and shopkeepers as to politicians. The only live witness was Stephan F. Meschutt, Supervisor of the Town of Southampton, who was called by the Commissioner for the purpose of demonstrating the extent to which Republican politicians intervened in traffic cases. While acknowledging that he had left a good number of traffic tickets with the clerk of Judge Kammerer's court, which was on the floor below that of the Supervisor's office, he vehemently denied doing so for the purpose of "fixing tickets," and asserted that he had simply left them "to the judgment of the judge." This prompted the Commissioner to ask, "Why didn't you tell these people to go downstairs with the tickets themselves, that you were-n't doing anything for them?" While the Supervisor's testimony which provoked the Commissioner's inquiry was transparently disin-genuous, his answer to that question had the ring of undisguised truth: "I guess maybe you've never been a supervisor."[16]

———◆———

Our new District Attorney had begun the selection of the scan-dals grand jury on June 4th, presenting them with a list of 413 names to be checked by them for persons they might know. In his initial ad-dress to the prospective grand jurors, Mr. Percy made a point of re-minding them that the order of the Governor which established the Extraordinary Special and Trial Term of the Supreme Court of which the grand jury would be a part was "very, very broad" and covered "any crime committed in the county." Subsequently, each prospec-tive juror he questioned was asked whether he approved of the stat-utes which made bookmaking a crime.[17]

On June 5th, for reasons neither indicated nor obvious, he asked some of the prospective jurors whether they had ever appeared be-fore any Congressional committee, and whether they were in any way involved in any state or federal inquiries referable to subver-sion.[18] In spite of these forays into the mysterious, the jury was completed on June 6th,[19] and by the last week in June, it was ready to get down to business.

———◆———

On June 26th, William S. Hart, whom Commissioner Shapiro had charged the preceding fall with *sub rosa* furniture-dealer dealings with the county while he had been on the county payroll, made a volun-tary appearance before the scandals grand jury in connection with the first matter it would consider. His attorney, Doug Brown, was inventive in his public statement on behalf of his client: "He accepted the position of assistant county director of Civil Defense as a civic duty and responsibility. There was no intent to defraud."[20] The fol-lowing week, Hart and four others involved in the conspiracy to hide the fact that Hart was selling furniture to the county were indicted on charges of perjury, subornation of perjury and conspiracy, as well as on Hart's act which underlay the whole proceeding, i.e., his sale of furniture to the county. By the time of presentation of evidence to the grand jury, further investigation had uncovered transactions unknown to Commissioner Shapiro at the time of his pre-election day publicity release the preceding fall. The indictments covered some $30,000 of furniture.[21]

————— ◆ —————

On July 9th, the JP removal proceeding continued with the cases of Charles F. Pfeifle of Babylon and Lester H. Davis of Brookhaven. As in the case of Rudy Kammerer, Royden Klein stipulated into the record the testimony accumulated by the Commissioner, called no witnesses on behalf of his clients, and took the position that no wrongdoing had been committed. The proceeding was continued to September 24th for the hearing regarding Clarence Duffield of Brookhaven, who had suffered a heart attack earlier in the summer.[22]

On July 16th, the extraordinary grand jury began to receive evidence concerning possible protection afforded by county officials to bookmaking and other gambling activities;[23] and then on August 7th following a recess, continued this inquiry.[24]

On August 30th, the extraordinary grand jury indicted J. Milford Kirkup, our Commissioner of Public Welfare, on charges of conspiring to misuse the county's name and credit. The indictment charged that Mr. Kirkup allowed Freistadt's, a prominent drug store establishment in Bay Shore, in the Town of Islip, to purchase antibiotics in the name of the Suffolk Home at Yaphank, which enabled the drug store to take advantage of the large discount which drug companies normally gave to state, county and other municipal agencies.[25]

On September 5th, Commissioner Shapiro issued a statement in which he charged that Arthur B. Smith, Chief Inspector of Building and Zoning for the town of Islip since 1950 had engaged in bribery and extortion in his dealings with builders who required building department approval for their construction, amassing $115,000 in realty holdings on a salary of $6,500. Further, according to the Commissioner, when Mr. Smith had appeared at the Commissioner's office that day, he took the Fifth Amendment in response to a question from the Commissioner, the Commissioner thereupon demanded he resign, and Mr. Smith handed him his resignation, to be delivered to the Islip Town Board, citing poor health as the reason for his action.[26]

The same day, Ford Hughes issued a statement about the Kirkup indictments. He started off by asserting that in indicting the Commissioner of Public Welfare the grand jury had likely been "misled or they became unwilling tools of the prosecutor". He then asked a question which, to those not totally on our side, might have seemed somewhat revealing. He said that he wanted to know why "the person or persons who told this fantastic story waited until it became politically expedient to talk." He then went on to report that some of the grand jurors "have been annoyed with Percy and so told him, for 'leaking' jury room discussions to newspaper reporters." Our Leader did not explain how he came to have information about the grand jury proceedings which, ultimately, could have come only from one or more of the grand jurors or a court official or employee assigned to the grand jury.[27]

On September 6th, John P. Cohalan, Jr., Islip Town Supervisor, received the resignation of Arthur B. Smith as Building Inspector, and immediately appointed Arthur G. Dickerson as Acting Building Inspector. Mr. Cohalan stated that Mr. Smith had resigned on the advice of his doctor, adding that it was well known that Mr. Smith had been in poor health for two years. Mr. Smith, after a brief meeting with Mr. Cohalan, unequivocally denied Commissioner Shapiro's charges.[28] Immediately beneath this report, in an untitled item, the *Times* recorded that Adrian Mason, the Democratic County Leader, had opined that Mr. Hughes' remarks about the extraordinary grand jury and the Kirkup indictment were disgraceful.[29]

On September 19th, the Commissioner issued a report to the Governor concerning the rental of trucks by the Suffolk County Highway Department. For years, the Highway Department, which rented many of the trucks it used in its operations, had rented them from its own foremen. In a 1953 report for the years 1951 and 1952, the State Department of Audit and Control had pointed out that this rental arrangement with the Department's employees was prohibited by section 412 of the state's County Law, which provided that no officer or employee of a county "shall be interested, directly or indirectly, in any claim, account or demand against or contract with the county." What the Commissioner discovered was that thirteen foremen were presently renting to the Department through dummy owners, such as relatives and friends--a practice that stopped as a consequence of his investigation of the Department. The *Times'* description of the Commissioner's report does not indicate whether it addressed the matter of possible financial loss to the county by reason of its now disconinued practice.[30]

On September 21, a *Times* editorial entitled "MR. SHAPIRO'S TENACITY" noted that in February, it had articulated its assumption that Mr. Shapiro would direct his attention impartially to Democratic and Republican local administrations, and lamented that this had not eventuated. While acknowledging that Mr. Shapiro had delved into other counties and the State Liquor Authority, it observed that these too were Republican bailiwicks. Noting that it was approaching two years since he had been appointed, the Times wondered if Mr. Shapiro was ever going to go anywhere else than Suffolk County, even to Democratic preserves.[31]

On September 25th, the Commissioner made the newspapers by announcing that no new investigations would be started until after Election Day. The Commissioner took the occasion to observe that the achievements of his office had been accomplished by a staff that by reason of his office's budget was limited to three investigators. What the Commissioner forgot to point out was that there were only three persons on his staff who were officially designated as investigators. If he had thought of it, he would have pointed out that the numerous lawyers attached to his office on a permanent and *ad hoc* basis did most of the important work in the investigations.[32]

On September 27th, the Commissioner released a report to the Governor in which, as reported by the *Times*, he accused John G. Carter, a foreman in the Highway Department of the Town of Southampton, of using Department employees on Department time to help him build his house (which the Commissioner said Mr. Carter admitted), build a 500-foot road leading to it, and repair his commercial fishing boat; and he stated that Mr. Carter had admitted accepting kickbacks from bulldozer owners who rented their equipment for road repair.[33]

On October 3rd, Inspector Francis D. J. Phillips, one of the most decorated officers in the history of the New York City Police Department, quite unexpectedly filed for retirement.[34] On October 5th, Inspector Phillips was indicted on a charge of Perjury in the First Degree. The indictment grew out of Inspector Phillips' testimony before the extraordinary grand jury on July 17th, when the grand jury was considering whether bookmakers and operators of gambling establishments had received protection from county officials. The testimony of Inspector Phillips which gave rise to the perjury charge had to do with protection of the Star Island Casino in Montauk, a gambling casino which had been raided and closed by state police the preceding summer after being in operation only a few months.[35]

On the same day, the extraordinary grand jury handed up indictments against John and Edna Britting, and Albert Glass. The three of them were indicted on one count of conspiracy. John Britting was also indicted on twelve counts of taking bribes, twelve counts of taking unlawful fees while a county officer, five counts of extortion, and four counts of having an unlawful interest in a contract with the county while a county officer. Glass was indicted on twelve counts of giving bribes. Edna Britting was indicted on three counts of assisting John to take bribes and three additional counts of assisting her husband take unlawful fees. Simultaneously, Harold B Meinhardt, a resident of Center Moriches, in the Town of Brookhaven, filed a taxpayer's suit on behalf of Suffolk county against the Brittings, Glass and eight others to recover the sum of $500,000 for losses presumably sustained by the county as a consequence of John Britting's sales of exclusive options on tax lien properties.[36]

On October 16th, the hearings in the removal proceeding against the five Justices of the Peace ended. The Appellate Division itself had conducted the hearing on Clarence Duffield, and then heard arguments from counsel, because Judge Adel had himself suffered a heart attack during the summer, and it was not clear as to just when he might be able to return to his duties as referee. Commissioner Shapiro argued that the JP's were unfit to hold public office. Messrs. Walser and Klein contended that none of the JP's had violated the law.[37]

On October 18th, Commissioner Shapiro issued a report to the Governor in which he asserted that every Town of Islip building department inspector appointed prior to January 1, 1956, had admitted accepting gratuities from builders; and, that some FHA inspectors had also engaged in the practice; that $105 per house was the standard exaction, necessarily increasing the price of each house and effecting an extortion in that amount from the purchasers. The Commissioner concluded that these payments explained the many allegations of homeowners concerning poor materials and construction and consequent road and cellar flooding. The Commissioner requested that the facts he had developed be forwarded to the District Attorney of Suffolk County and the United States Attorney.[38]

On October 20th, Arthur G. Dickerson, Acting Town Building Inspector of the town of Islip since the resignation of Arthur B. Smith the previous month, took the refreshingly direct approach of describing the Commissioner's charges as a "direct and unmitigated lie," and demanded an opportunity to testify before the grand jury about the matter. Mr. Dickerson acknowledged that he had received "'unsolicited Christmas gifts of liquor or its equivalent' from builders." He commented, "If this constituted graft, then everyone is a criminal." He went on to deny that he had ever accepted a bribe.[39]

On October 23rd, the extraordinary grand jury handed up two indictments against A. Russell Richards, the Chief Investigator of the District Attorney's office. One of them consisted of one count of perjury, stemming from Richards' testimony before the Special Grand Jury on August 7th. The other consisted of fourteen counts of bribery, representing a bribe allegedly taken during each of fourteen successive months commencing with November, 1952, which Mr. Percy explained that these indictments reflected the grand jury's judgment that Mr. Richards had received bribes for insulating gamblers from the criminal process. The District Attorney had a prepared statement for the press, in which, after noting that the perjury indictment could result in imprisonment for five years, and that the bribery indictment could represent a possible one hundred forty years, he presented, in his customary non-political way, the background of the indictments, i.e., that everyone knew that this had been going on for years.[40]

On the same day, the grand jury also handed up a two-count willful neglect of duty indictment against Philipp A. Hattemer, chairman of the Suffolk County Board of Supervisors; an indictment charging his wife, Miriam, with first degree perjury; and, an indictment charging John G. Carter, the Southampton Highway Department foreman who had been investigated by Commissioner Shapiro, with perjury, extortion and the receipt of an illegal fees.[41]

The basis for the two misdemeanor counts against Phil Hattemer was that he had allowed county department heads to make purchases of more than $1,000 without competitive bidding. The District Attorney explained to the press that Mr. Hattemer's conduct had cost the taxpayers $130,000 during the period December, 1954 - December, 1955.[42] The basis for the felony indictment against Miriam Hattemer was her testimony, before the Commissioner of Investigation, as to where she obtained the money, $219.68, for her purchase of a one-third interest in a tax-lien redemption in May, 1952. (The acquisition had made the newspapers one month previously, when Adrian Mason, Chairman of the Suffolk County Democratic Committee, charged at a political rally in Kings Park, that Phil and Miriam had used a dummy, one James S. Fuoco, a Patchogue liquor store owner, to purchase the one-third interest. According to Mr. Mason, the value of the entire parcel of property, for which the amount paid the County Treasurer for redemption of the tax lien was $654, was now $30,000.[43])[44]

The extortion indictment of Carter was referable to that portion of the Commissioner of Investigation's report which accused him of accepting kickbacks from bulldozer owners who rented their equipment for road repair. The perjury indictment was based on Carter's grand jury testimony that the money he had received from these people had been voluntary contributions to the Republican Party.[45]

———— ◆ ————

In the meantime, the Republican candidate for District Attorney, John P. Cohalan, Jr., was enjoying himself on the campaign trail. He was having a good time tweaking the noses of the Commissioner of Investigation, the District Attorney of Suffolk County, and the Chairman of the Suffolk County Democratic Committee. Noting that ticket fixing had probably been around "since Ben Hur rode his chariot in Rome", he would remind his audiences of the nineteen suspended sentences for which Southampton Justice of the Peace

Rudolph Kammerer had been upbraided and brought before the Appellate Division by Commissioner Shapiro. Then, with mock seriousness, Mr. Cohalan would tell his audiences that the Commissioner had forgotten No. 20. He would then waive with glee a photostatic copy of the one that George Percy, who had played basketball with Rudy Kammerer in high school, had obtained, after pleading guilty to doing sixty miles per hour on a local road.

Mr. Cohalan's second set piece had to do with Adrian Mason, Chairman of the Democratic County Committee of Suffolk County, and, in the administration of Governor Harriman, Deputy Commissioner of Motor Vehicles. It seems that one Patsy Tuccio had the misfortune to get three speeding tickets in eighteen months, which resulted in his driver's license being revoked with no reapplication for a license permitted for a year. However, Patsy had the good fortune to have Deputy Commissioner of Motor Vehicles Mason get it back for him in a month.[46]

———— ◆ ————

On November 9th, safely beyond Election Day, and therefore safely beyond election-campaign use of their action as an acknowledgment that it was overdue, the Board of Supervisors voted the money to establish a county purchasing department.[47]

On November 16th, the extraordinary grand jury handed up indictments against Stephan F. Meschutt, Supervisor of the Town of Southampton, and Edward C. (Babe) Freres, First Deputy County Clerk, who had just won election to the town office of Receiver of Taxes for the Town of Huntington. Mr. Meschutt was charged with disregarding the statute prohibiting a county official from serving as a director of a bank that was a depository for county funds. What Mr. Freres and his wife, Marie, had done was to purchase tax liens on two parcels, the larger of which was intended to serve as a gift of a house building plot to their daughter and her husband. The owner of the larger plot had subsequently exercised his right to redeem his land within three years by paying to Babe the accrued back taxes, charges and interest; and the smaller parcel was found to be owned by the State of New York, which had forgotten to file its tax deed to the property. Babe now found himself charged with having involved himself "in a claim and account and demand against and contract" with the county while he was an official of the county, a prohibited act under the state's County Law.[48]

The grand jury did not hand up any other indictments that day. However, New York City Police Department Inspector Francis Phillips, indicted the previous month on one count of perjury in the first degree, applied to Justice Tilzer for an order dismissing the indictment, or, in the alternative for permission to inspect the grand jury minutes.[49]

———————◆◆———————

On December 2nd, Commissioner Shapiro submitted to the Governor and the press his report on Henry Schmidt, Superintendent of the Dix Hills Water District and President of the Dix Hills Republican Club. The Commissioner accused Henry of mulcting the taxpayers of the Town of Huntington out of thousands of dollars in tap-in fees, the fees for connecting new users to the water district's water mains; and, that he had not paid federal or State income taxes on the income.[50]

A water district in New York State is essentially a municipal water company for a described geographical area. Dix Hills lies in the southern part of the town of Huntington. At issue were fees Henry had been collecting from developers for connecting their newly constructed homes on private roads, i.e., on roads not yet dedicated to the town, on his own time, using non-water district equipment, to water mains which had not yet been accepted by the water district, i.e., to water mains still owned by the developers.[51]

Henry maintained that the money was legitimately his; and, that he had performed the services and accepted the fees for them only after being advised by the attorney for the water district that it was all right for him to do so.[52] He noted that he had shown the Commissioner's investigator his income tax returns for 1955, the first year in which he had done this work, which showed the 1955 income for that work, $260; and, that it was not yet time to file his returns for the tax year 1956, which would show the $1,300 he had earned for that work in 1956.[53] Henry turned the entire sum of $1,560 over to the the town Board with the request that it be held in escrow pending a determination as to his right to the money.[54]

Joseph Cermak, Supervisor of the Town of Huntington, said that the town board resolution appointing Henry in 1954 was not clear on fees paid by developers; and so, he appointed a committee to look into the matter, and wrote to the Attorney General for an opinion on the matter.[55]

Henry and all the members of the Huntington Town Board were subpoenaed to appear before the Extraordinary Special and Trial Term grand jury on December 6th, where all of them signed waivers of immunity. Also appearing before the grand jury was Charles H. Stoll, the lawyer who had formed and then served as counsel to the Dix Hills Water District until 1955, when the town board decided that the district had progressed to the point where the board should manage it and the town attorney represent it. On December 11th, Mr. Stoll appeared before the town board and characterized the Commissioner's charges as "unfounded and ridiculous," pointing out that all the work done by Henry had been that for which the developers were responsible.[56] Presumably, to the extent he was permitted to do so, Mr. Stoll had given the grand jury a tutorial on what's what with developers and water districts when he appeared before that information-seeking body. Nonetheless, on December 18th, the grand jury handed up a presentment to Justice Tilzer in which it "severely censured and condemned" Henry for keeping the money, and the entire Republican Huntington Town Board for allowing him to do so. It praised Commissioner Shapiro for "well serving the public."[57] The grand jury, as guided by Mr. Percy, apparently did not see any inconsistency between the certitude with which it chastised Henry and the Town Board and applauded the Commissioner, on one hand, and its request for an adjudication as to whether Henry was entitled to the fees he had placed in escrow with the town board the Commissioner's report, on the other.

On December 17th, all five of the justices of the peace in the removal proceeding before the Appellate Division sub- mitted their resignations to their respective town clerks. According to Guy Walser, the reason Moses Drake resigned was that he "couldn't endure the anxiety and uncertainty of waiting for the court's decision any longer." He added that Judge Drake had told him that he was "not conscious of any wrongdoing" on his part as a justice of the peace. Royden Klein gave no reason for the resignations of his clients. Ever dispassionate, Commissioner Shapiro quickly issued a statement, in which he referred to the resignations as "the greatest mass resignation of justices in the whole judicial history of this state"; declared that "whatever the Appellate Division's ultimate decision may be on this concerted effort to deprive it of jurisdiction, these eleventh-hour resignations under fire cannot prevent a justifiable finding of guilt by the court of public opinion"; and characterized the resignations as "merely a bow to the inevitable."[58]

On December 18th, William H. Fry, Suffolk County Clerk was indicted on misdemeanor charges of willful neglect of duty and paying fraudulent claims against the county, arising out of his auditing and subsequent payment of bills of more than $4,000 for supplies which had been purchased by other officials without competitive bidding.[59]

On December 21st, the Appellate Division, confirming Commissioner Shapiro's fears, dismissed his removal proceeding against the justices of the peace, finding that the JP's resignations had rendered the proceeding moot.[60]

On December 31st, we ushered out the old year by appointing a Director of Purchases for our new county purchasing department.[61]

Notes

1. "Democrats Back Percy," *New York Times*, March 24, 1956.
2. "3D Shapiro Study Sent to Suffolk," ibid., March 30, 1956.
3. "Shapiro Charges Go To Appellate Unit," ibid., April 12, 1956
4. "Special Court Term Asked For Suffolk," ibid., April 26, 1956.
5. "Shapiro Accuses 2 More In Suffolk," ibid., May 4, 1956,
6. "Governor Orders Suffolk Inquiry Under Democrat," ibid., May 5, 1956.
7. Ibid.
8. "Shapiro Charges Britting Shared in Suffolk 'Deal'," *New York Times*, May 11, 1956.
9. "Suffolk Inquiry Opened by Court," ibid., May 12, 1956.
10. "Britting Accused in New Land Deal," ibid., May 21, 1956.

11. "Adel to Referee Suffolk Inquiry," ibid., June 2, 1956.

12. 2 G.O.P. Leaders Accused in Courtroom," ibid., June 19, 1956.

13. "Fixing of Ticket Denied by Crews," ibid., June 20, 1956.

14. "Suffolk Justice Fails to Testify," ibid., June 21, 1956.

15. Ibid.

16. "Jurist Is Silent on Ticket-Fixing," New York Times, June 26, 1956.

17. "Suffolk Inquiry on Graft Starts," ibid., June 5, 1956.

18. Clayton Knowles, "Percy Questions 4 on Subversion," ibid., June 6, 1956.

19. "Suffolk Inquiry Completes Panel," ibid., June 7, 1956.

20. "Suffolk Jury Hears Testimony by Hart," ibid., June 27, 1956.

21. "Five Are Indicted by Suffolk Jury," ibid., July 3, 1956.

22. "2 More Jurists of Suffolk Silent as State Charges Ticket Fixing," ibid., July 10, 1956.

23. "7 Witnesses Heard on Suffolk Gaming," ibid., July 17, 1956.

24. "Suffolk Jury Reconvenes," ibid., August 8, 1956.

25. "4 Accused in Use of Suffolk Name," ibid., August 31, 1956.

26. "Islip Aide Quits in State Inquiry," ibid., September 6, 1956.

27. "Grand Jury Reported Annoyed," ibid.

28. "New Building Aide Appointed in Islip," ibid, September 7, 1956.

29. [Untitled], ibid.

30. Lathmond Robinson, Jr., "Graft in Hiring of Trucks Is Laid to 13 Suffolk Aides," New York Times, September 20, 1956. (Inquiry at the New York State Library discloses that Commissioner Shapiro's report is no longer in its files.)

31. Editorial, ibid., September 21, 1956.

32. "Shapiro Rejects New Inquiry Bids." ibid., September 26, 1956.

33. "Foreman Accused on Suffolk Work," ibid., September 28, 1956.

34. Ira Henry Freeman, "Suffolk Indicts Police Inspector, 3 Others Indicted," ibid., October 6, 1956.

35. Joseph C. Ingraham, "Police Hero Quits Abruptly; Testified in Suffolk Inquiry," ibid., October 4, 1956.

36. Ira Henry Freeman, "Suffolk Indicts Police Inspector," ibid., October 6, 1956.

37. "Court Ends Hearing in Suffolk 'Fixing'," ibid., October 17, 1956.

38. "Inspectors Accused of Graft in Suffolk." ibid., October 19, 1956.

39. "Accused Islip Aide Hits Shapiro Report," ibid., October 21, 1956.

40. "Jury in Suffolk Indicts Official," ibid., October 24, 1956.

41. "Suffolk Indicts Top Supervisor," ibid., October 26, 1956.

42. Ibid.

43. "Suffolk Official Backs Land Deal," *New York Times*, September 26, 1956.

44. "Suffolk Indicts Top Supervisor," ibid., October 26, 1956.

45. Ibid.

46. See "Eisenhower Rated With Washington And Lincoln Here," *Long Islander*, October 25, 1956.

47. "Record Budget for Suffolk," *New York Times*, November 10, 1956.

48. "2 More Indicted By Suffolk Jury," ibid., November 17, 1956.

49. Ibid.

50. "Fraud Charged in Suffolk Fees," *New York Times*, December 3, 1956.

51. "Attorney General Asked for Opinion on Schmidt Charges," *Long Islander*, December 6, 1956

52. Ibid.

53. "Town Board Before Suffolk Grand Jury on Schmidt Charges," *Long Islander*, December 6, 1956.

54. "Suffolk Aide Backs Right to Water Fee," *New York Times*, December 6, 1956; and "Attorney General Asked For Opinion on Schmidt Charges," *Long Islander*, December 6, 1956.

55. "Attorney General Asked For Opinion on Schmidt Charges," *Long Islander*, December 6, 1956.

56. "Stoll Denounces Charges Against Henry Schmidt," ibid., December 13, 1956.

57. "Town Board Censured By Grand Jury in Probe of Hills Water District, Ibid., December 20, 1956.

58. Laythmond Robinson, Jr., "5 Suffolk Jurists Quit in "Fix" Case As Verdict Nears," *New York Times*, December 18, 1956.

59. "Neglect Charged to Suffolk Clerk," ibid., December 19, 1956.

60. "Court Drops Action on Peace Justices," ibid., December 22, 1956.

61. "Chief of Purchasing Named for Suffolk," ibid., January 1, 1957.

Chapter 5

In the meantime, President Eisenhower, running for re-election, had racked up an awesome plurality in Suffolk County, and John Cohalan would be the county's District Attorney on January 1, 1957.

As expected, the Governor received a letter from the Extraordinary Special and Trial Term grand jury beseeching him to do everything in his power to retain Mr. Percy as the person in charge of its proceedings.[1] It need not be said that John Cohalan was not going to resign as soon as he took office so that the Governor could appoint the man he had just defeated to have his job. The Governor's position was if there was anyone who should not handle the special grand jury, it would be John.[2]

By the time 1957 arrived, it had become clear to George Percy that he was not going to be named as special prosecutor; and so, quite properly, he deposited the three file cabinets-full of his papers relating to the Extraordinary Special and Trial Term grand jury in a vault in the Suffolk County National Bank, in Riverhead, to await the appointment of whoever would be getting the assignment. John Cohalan, never bashful, asked George Percy for the keys. Ever the soul of tact, when he quite properly declined to hand over the keys, given the uncertainty as to who would handle the special grand jury, George could not resist saying to John, "I think it would be most unwise of me to permit you to inform yourself about such matters."[3]

———— ♦ ————

The Governor and Attorney General Jacob Javits ultimately agreed upon Edward E. Rigney, a partner in the Manhattan law firm of Alexander and Green, as the new special prosecutor.[4] There is nothing known to the writer to suggest that the *New York Times'* reference to him, upon his appointment on January 5th, as "an independent Democrat," which suggests the absence of a participatory relationship with the Democratic Party organization, was anything but accurate. (If he had been referred to as "a reform Democrat", then, in the parlance of New York City politics, he would have been a person affirmatively allied with the Party but in the camp opposed to Carmine DeSapio, then the leader of Tammany Hall.)

———— ♦ ————

Edward Rigney was born in upstate New York Ontario County in 1908. He graduated from Hobart College in 1931, and began law school at Columbia University, leaving in the Depression year of 1933 to manage the family store in Holcombe in upstate New York, ultimately graduating from Fordham Law School in 1936. He would serve as an assistant U.S. Attorney for the Southern District of New York. In World War II, he enlisted in the U.S. Army as a private, and was a captain in military intelligence at the end of the war. Following the war, he served as a member of the staff of Major General Telford Taylor, the United States Chief of Counsel at the Nuremburg War Crimes Trials. He then returned to the U.S. Attorney's office. In 1950, having served briefly as a deputy New York City Police Commissioner, he joined Alexander and Green.[5]

———— ♦ ————

John Cohalan's comment, though disingenuous concerning his own non-selection, was manly and professional concerning Mr. Rigney: "I still think the job should be mine, since I was elected by an overwhelming majority of the people of Suffolk County. But Mr.

Rigney is assured that I will give him every cooperation." Ever gracious George Percy's comment was that he knew "nothing of Mr. Rigney's ability, experience or force of purpose."[6] When Mr. Rigney held a press conference two days after his appointment, he was asked if he intended to appoint Mr. Percy to his staff. The answer was that he "would not exclude" the former District Attorney from consideration.[7]

At the press conference, Mr. Rigney distributed a prepared statement. Like any other statement prepared for the press, it was intended for the widest possible dissemination in its most complete form as penned. While the *Times* only quoted snippets from it, the *Long Islander* appears to have set forth all eleven paagraphs of it at length. The first paragraph, though self-congratulatory, was neutral enough. Also, it must be conceded that, standing alone, the fourth paragraph was a model of decorum: "It would be inappropriate for me at this time to make any comment on any individual case and I do not intend to do so." Unfortunately, the fourth paragraph was preceded by the second paragraph, in which he took the occasion to point out that twenty-four indictments had already been returned against "more than a score of defendants," numbering among them "several present or former public officials."; and, by the third, in which he enumerated, "among others", the crimes specified by the indictments.[8]

———— ◆ ————

On January 10th, Commissioner Shapiro was the principal speaker at a National Democratic Club luncheon in Manhattan. He took the occasion to castigate the New York City area newspapers for "doing a miserable job" in its reporting of the results of his investigations in Suffolk County. He cited as the most recent example of the press' non-reporting of Suffolk County Republicans' disrespect for the law its failure to report the fact that on December 27th, District Attorney-elect John Cohalan had "started upon his work by publicly thumbing his nose at the law he was sworn to uphold." According to Mr. Shapiro, Mr. Cohalan demonstrated his lack of respect for the law by having gone to "a man under indictment" to take his oath of office. It appears that John Cohalan, Alex Jaeger, the new County

Clerk, and Charles R. Dominy, the new Sheriff, all went to the retiring County Clerk, William H. Fry, who was under indictment for neglect of duty and payment of fraudulent claims.[9] The Commissioner of Investigation did not bother to tell his non-partisan good government audience that the oath of office is the same for every office holder in the state and is taken by a notary public if no public officer is around to do it. If one's public office was one which anyone but your family would be likely to be aware of, you would probably have access to the County Clerk himself as the oath-taking official. You had to go to the County Clerk's office no matter who took your oath, however, since all oaths of office had to be filed in the County Clerk's office. Possibly, the Commissioner, in his unfavorable estimate of John Cohalan's fitness for the position of District Attorney, also had in mind that to which he also made reference in apparently shocked seriousness, viz., that in the lobby of the county courthouse in which the county clerk's office was housed, there stood a Christmas tree. On the Christmas tree was an ornament. The ornament was a figure hung in effigy and labeled "Shapiro". As the Commissioner told the story, Mr. Fry administered the oaths of office right in front of the tree in the courthouse lobby. (According to courthouse personnel, the oaths were administered in a separate room.)[10]

On January 21st, the Governor sent to the State Senate for confirmation three nominations for judicial positions, one of them being that of Irwin Shapiro for Justice of the City Court of New York City.[11] (The City Court was the New York City analogue of the county court for civil matters in counties outside of New York City.) By virtue of his yeoman's work in his quest, Mr. Shapiro apparently had become entitled to the next opening on the bench in Queens County. In its story, the Times reported that "Governor Harriman is known to have been displeased with some of Mr. Shapiro's earlier reports and with some features of his conduct of the Suffolk County investigation." The slickness of the suggestion on behalf of the Governor that he did not approve of all aspects of the way in which the Commissioner had comported himself or of all his reports, innocently published by the Times, was admired by us, to whom it seemed clear that what the Governor disapproved of was being associated with his party's game plan for decreasing the Republican pluralities in burgeoning Suffolk County.

———— ◆ ————

In the same week, John Cohalan, who had delighted partisan Republican audiences with his anecdotes about ticket-fixing--as well as by his vigorous declamations that the scandals investigations constituted a war against the Republican Party in Suffolk County--decided to have some fun with the Shapiro charges and the Hattemer indictments concerning purchases of over $1,000 that had not been made through competitive bidding. He sent a letter to his predecessor in office concerning payment of bills submitted by a lumber company in connection with work done on the District Attorney's office in Bay Shore the preceding fall. The letter, which he distributed to the county's weekly papers, set forth his understanding that the original bill for the work, as first submitted in October, 1956, was for $1,436.41, but upon the suggestion of someone in the office of the then District Attorney, had been resubmitted as three separate bills. Given the requirement for competitive bidding for purchases in excess of $1,000 (as distinguished from $2,500 for a public works contract), John, citing the relevant statute, wondered if the advertisement requirement for the work to be done had been fulfilled, and asked George for his clarification of the matter so that he could approve payment of the bills.[12]

When George Percy was contacted, his comment was, "I could not reply to that letter without using unprintable language."[13] Poor, humorless George! He could have had as much fun with John Cohalan as John was having with him, given the lightness of John's confection of official concern that marked his letter. After all, if renovation of a county office did not amount to a public works contract, as distinguished from a purchase by the county (no matter that the bills included charges for the purchase of materials), it would be hard to imagine what would be a public works contract. At the same time, the new District Attorney's letter did raise the issue of someone intentionally rigging the billing to avoid the issue of the requirement of competitive bidding. Both Commissioner Shapiro's charges of illegal non-use of competitive bidding for purchases of more than $1,000 and Phil Hattemer's indictments based on other officials' non-use of the bidding process for such purchases were based on the Commissioner's and George Percy's interpretation of what constituted a purchase of more than $1,000.

———————— ◆ ————————

On March 17th, Mr. Rigney announced the appointment of Edwyn Silberling, who had been serving as an assistant district attorney in Frank Hogan's office since 1951, as a special assistant attorney general.[14]

On May 2nd, Frank Costello, who had co-starred with Senator Charles W. Tobey of New Hampshire in the Kefauver Committee hearings in New York City in 1951, was shot in the head, though not fatally. When the police arrived at the scene of the attempted assassination, they discovered a slip of paper with the notation, "casino wins". Neither the New York City Police Department nor Mr. Rigney ever indicated whether this memorandum was thought to be a reference to casino winnings, a reference to the underworld figure, Frank Casino (who had already appeared three times before the grand jury in connection with casino gambling in Suffolk County), or both. However, on May 12th, Mr. Rigney informed the press that the special grand jury was about to reconvene; and that when it did, its first witness would be Mr. Casino.[15]

On May 13th, William S. Hart and his friends who had enabled him to sell furniture to the county while he was on the county payroll as deputy civil defense director pleaded guilty to their indictments; and Mr. Rigney indicated that he would kill other pending indictments against them, stating that there was "no evidence that the county was overcharged in any of the transactions nor [sic] that the county failed to receive the item for which it paid."[16]

On May 27th, the Appellate Division of the Supreme Court dismissed the indictment of Supervisor Stephan Meschutt and those against Commissioner of Welfare Milford Kirkup.[17] On June 2nd, Mr. Rigney announced that he would "accept as final" the dismissal of the Meschutt indictment, but had not yet decided whether he would appeal the court's dismissal of those against Commissioner Kirkup.[18] This was eminently reasonable on both counts. It would have been most unlikely that anyone could have gotten the Court of Appeals to overrule the Appellate Division in the Meschutt case, for the Appellate Division's opinion in that case spelled out what should have been clear to George Percy--it was clear to just about everyone else--before he ever thought of bringing the indictment against Meschutt, namely that under the controlling statutes there was no basis for Supervisor Meschutt's actions to constitute a crime.[19] However, the syllogisms forming the Appellate Division's opinion regarding the Kirkup indictments implicitly acknowledged the possibility that a different view of the undisputed material facts might be taken by the Court of Appeals. Moreover, the Appellate Division went out of its way to condemn that which Commissioner Kirkup had permitted to be done by the favored druggist, notwithstanding its view of the legal sufficiency of the indictments under the controlling statutes.[20] Thus, the special prosecutor undoubtedly felt that he had an affirmative obligation to seek permission of the Court of Appeals to appeal from the dismissals of the Kirkup indictments.

On June 3rd, the Appellate Division unanimously dismissed the neglect of duty indictment against Phillip Hattemer, on the basis of well established law that in order to establish criminal liability for a public official's failure to perform a duty enjoined by law--in this case the duty of the Chairman of the Board of supervisors to see to it that all laws are faithfully executed by county officials--the neglect had to be willful and intentional, which, in this case presupposed actual knowledge that purchases of food by the county's Department of Welfare and its tuberculosis Sanitarium were not made in accordance with notice and bidding requirements.[21]

The next day, at the weekly meeting of the Huntington Town Board, Supervisor Cermak disclosed that the Attorney General had notified the town that Henry Schmidt was entitled to the water-tapping fees for which he had been condemned by the special grand jury and which he had placed in escrow the preceding December.[22]

On June 6th, Hart was fined $2,500 and placed on probation for five years; one of his friends was fined $500 and placed on probation for one year; a second friend was put on probation for one year; and the third accomplice received a straight suspended sentence without probation.[23]

On June 26th, Commissioner Kirkup dismissed Deputy Commissioner of Welfare Serge Bessaraboff, who had testified before the Extraordinary Special and Trial Term grand jury in connection with the use of the Department of Public Welfare by Freistadt's Drug Store to buy drugs at the institutional rate. Mr. Bessaraboff claimed that he was dismissed because his testimony was damaging to the Commissioner; and Mr. Rigney announced that he was going to look into the matter.[24] On July 9th, Mr. Rigney issued a statement which began by labelling as a "lame excuse" the Commissioner's explanation that Mr. Bessaraboff had been let go because the Commissioner had found his work to be unsatisfactory, and in which he went on to characterize the discharge as "an act of vengeance" and "an act of revenge" in retaliation for Mr. Bessaraboff's grand jury testimony, as well as a threat to other witnesses. He assured Mr. Bessaraboff and all other witnesses, past and prospective, of of his support, and invited information concerning retaliation of witnesses.[25]

It is quite possible that Bessaraboff was sacked because of his testimony. It is also quite possible that he had known that he was going to be sacked before he ever testified before the grand jury. (People in non-civil service protected positions, even ones in which the staffing of which has a political component, are sometimes let go because they simply can't handle the job.) It is unknown whether Mr. Bessaraboff volunteered his testimony to the special prosecutor or simply told the truth when called upon to testify before the grand jury. It is a certainty that Mr. Rigney's position in the matter was either a reflection or an extrapolation of Bessaraboff's story. It is also a certainty that in the process of waging political as well as prosecutorial warfare in the press, Mr. Rigney was making highly prejudicial statements about a defendant he would be prosecuting if he successfully appealed the Appellate Division's dismissal of the Kirkup indictments.

On July 15th, the Appellate Division, by a 3-2 vote, the dissenters not filing an opinion, dismissed the perjury indictment against Miriam Hattemer. The majority opinion, after a discussion of the evidence which it described as "the crux of the prosecution's case", concluded that "a finding would not be proper that the defendant testified falsely, willfully and knowingly in Suffolk County concerning a material fact."[26]

On September 10th, the Board of Supervisors voted to create a county public works department.

On September 30th, the Extraordinary Special and Trial Term grand jury handed up two indictments against Fred W. Boergesson, Jr. Freddie Boergesson was a title searcher by trade, and at the time of his indictment, was a title searcher in the employ of the Suffolk County Department of Public Works. One of the indictments contained ten felony counts charging him with accepting bribes; the other, ten felony counts charging him with accepting illegal fees. Each of the bribery counts represented a maximum fine of $5,000 and ten-year prison term; and each of the illegal fees counts carried a maximum fine of $4,000 and a prison sentence of ten-years. The gravamen of the indictments was that in 1953 and 1954, when Freddie was an administrative assistant to the Suffolk County Board of Tax Arrears, he had accepted $8,000 from three real estate operators in consideration of his effecting favored treatment for them as bidders for tax sale properties.[27]

———— ◆ ————

Since 1957, being an odd-numbered year, presented no statewide election contests, each party was on its own in the general election. We won the only county-wide canvass, and we retained our 8-2 control of the Board of Supervisors. Yet, while we prevailed in the county race by the usual comfortable odd-year margin, our pluralities in the town elections were generally down. Since our county-wide count was not diminished, and since neither the Shapiro charges nor the Percy indictments were referable to towns, our smaller pluralities in town contests could reasonably be attributed to a growing unrest about escalating taxes. The increase was almost entirely attributable to the steep rise in school district taxes, over which the town governments had no control, because school expenditures and bond issues were the province of school districts, entities over which the town governments had no control. However, the school taxes were part of the bills issued by the towns.

More serious was the reality that we retained our 8-2 control of the Board of Supervisors only because we regained by a few votes the supervisorship of a small-electorate eastend town which we had lost by a few votes in 1955; for we lost the Huntington supervisorship by 94 votes out of 32,972 cast. The loss was not a matter of Huntington reflecting the most serious of the across-the-board reductions of our township office pluralities due to increasing, tax-caused voter discontent. The loss had to do with zoning.

Notes

1. "Harriman Moves to Keep Democrat on Suffolk Inquiry," *New York Times*, November 20, 1956
2. Ibid.
3. "Percy Keeps Papers on Suffolk Inquiry," *New York Times*, January 3, 1957.
4. "Javits Appoints Democrat to Head Suffolk Inquiry," ibid, January 6, 1957.
5. Wolfgang Saxon, "Edward E. Rigney, 85, a Lawyer and Ex-Federal Prosecutor, Dies," ibid., February 22, 1994
6. "Javits Appoints Democrat to Head Suffolk Inquiry," ibid., February 6, 1957.
7. "Impartial Inquiry in Suffolk Vowed," ibid., January 8, 1957.
8. "Rigney, Independent Democrat, Named Special Prosecutor," *Long Islander*, January 10,1957.
9. "Shapiro Upraids the Press on Suffolk; Says Indicted Man Gave Oath to Cohalan," *New York Times*, January 11, 1957.
10. Ibid.
11. Warren Weaver, Jr., "Harriman Appoints Shapiro City Judge," *New York Times*, January 22, 1957.
12. "Cohalan Demands Percy Explanation Of County Claims," *Long Islander*, January 24, 1957.
13. "Percy and Cohalan Deadlocked Over Payment of Bill," ibid., January 31, 1957.
14. "Ex-Aide of Hogan Joins Staff in Suffolk County," *New York Times*, March 18, 1957.
15. "Suffolk Jury to Call High Costello Aide," ibid., May 13, 1957.
16. "Four Admit Guilt in Suffolk Inquiry into Illegal Sales," ibid., May 14, 1957.

17. Appellate Division Decision Clears 2 in Suffolk," ibid., May 28, 1957.
18. "Suffolk Case Weighed," ibid., June 3, 1957.
19. *People v. Meschutt*, 3 A.D. 2d 938.
20. *People v. Kirkup*, 3 A.D 2d 937.
21. *People v. Hattemer*, 4 A.D. 2d 674.
22. "Dodge Endorsed," *Long Islander*, June 6, 1957.
23. "4 In Suffolk Get Suspended Term," *New York Times*, June 7, 1957.
24. "State Aide to Scan Suffolk Dismissal," ibid., June 28, 1957.
25. "Dismissal of Official in Suffolk is Called Revenge for Testimony," ibid., July 10, 1957.
26. *People v. Hattemer*, 4 A.D. 2d 775.
27. "Suffolk Aide Held on Bribery Charges," *New York Times*, October 1, 1957.

Chapter 6

Zoning, as an exercise of the inherent prerogative of a governing authority to use its police power--its power to regulate conduct for the public health, safety, morals or general welfare--goes back to colonial times in America. In New England in the 1600's, there were local land committees which had authority over uses of property for farming and structures. Examples of ordinances concerning buildings were those which prohibited wooden chimneys and thatch roofs as fire hazards. By the 1700's, there were laws governing the location of slaughterhouses and distilleries; and laws restricting the locations of various kinds of businesses proliferated during the 18th and 19th centuries.

The genesis of zoning in its modern sense, which comprehends the concept of overall planning by municipalities for the use of land, was the rapid and enormous increase in the population of urban areas in the latter part of the 19th century and the simultaneous expansion of all sorts of business, manufacturing and industrial uses in these urban centers. By the beginning of the 20th century, there was widespread use of ordinances restricting types of land uses and restrictions on lot size, set backs and height of structures; and by the 1920's, many cities and suburban municipalities had comprehensive zoning ordinances enacted pursuant to state enabling legislation, the validity of which had been upheld by state court decisions.

In 1926, the United States Supreme Court, citing some of these decisions with approval, held that this comprehensive type of zoning was constitutional, upholding it on the old common law theory of regulating a public nuisance. This judicial landmark opened the way for a nationwide effort to regulate the use of land. The most immediate impact of such laws was felt in those areas which had not already been blighted, that is to say, existing non-urban localities, and non-urban areas surrounding metropolitan areas which had begun to develop in earnest in the 1920's. The conception, implementation and enforcement of zoning ordinances as the instrumentality for the orderly arrangement of residential areas was perceived as a constructive social device. In legal contemplation, the upholding of the constitutionality of such laws was based on the specific inherent police power of the states, delegated to municipalities, to protect property. This kind of action by communities was perceived to be laudable, because its purpose was to preserve the aesthetic quality of, as well as the financial interest in residential areas. It was looked upon as a way of preserving the gains and status achieved by those who moved from residential surroundings that were not regarded as nice as those into which they were moving; and the urban immigrants to non-urban areas who constituted the great post-World War II exodus from the cities were precisely those who were most in favor of zoning ordinances. In Suffolk County, as the post-war residents of theretofore sparsely inhabited areas came to have a voice, ultimately the dominant one, in the affairs of these communities, they were the most vociferous defenders and advocates of strict enforcement of the zoning ordinances.

From the very beginning of the adoption of zoning ordinances, the statutes of New York and other states provided for zoning boards of appeals, which performed two basic functions. One was to enable a municipality to vary the requirements of a zoning ordinance in specific cases in order to preserve the ordinance's goals without being unreasonable. Examples of this function would be the determinations of requests for variances from the minimum area, side, rear or front lot requirements for the zone in which the property was situated. The other primary responsibility of a zoning board of appeals was to determine whether certain specific uses of land should be permitted, regardless of the zone in which the land lay, when the ordinance required an affirmative determination that the zoning ordinance's requirements for such a use had been met. Examples of this function would be a determination upon an application to build a shopping center or to operate or expand a sand pit.

Probably a good fifty per cent of the matters which came before the zoning board in Huntington (and probably in the other towns in the county which had any significant amount of this kind of activity), did not actually entail hearings in any adversarial sense. This was because anything that could not be approved by the town's Building Clerk as a prerequisite for her issuing a building permit had to be considered and passed upon by the Board following an open hearing. These hearings amounted to no more than the chairman announcing the application on the list of an evening's matters by reference to the applicant's name, the application number, the location of the property, and the nature of the relief requested. On this type of application, even the precise extent of the relief requested might not always be described in the announcement. Usually, the applicant himself, unaccompanied by a lawyer, would rise when his application was identified by his name, and when no one else got up in response to the chairman's question as to whether or not there was anyone present in favor of or opposed to the granting of the application, the applicant would be told by the chairman that he would hear from the board in due course.

Many times, in Huntington, no one would show up on this kind of application, because notice was required to be given by the applicant only to those property owners within two hundred feet of the boundaries of the property; and probably seventy-five per cent of all applicants on applications the granting of which required only minimal deviations from the zoning ordinance, would, on the advice of the Building Clerk, go around and get consents from their neighbors within the two hundred feet. There was always the possibility that a variance which did not offend the neighbors might not be good for the larger immediate area or that the granting of it might set an unwise precedent. However, the Board, or at least the chairman, usually had the benefit of any notes the Building Clerk would have made on the particular request for a building permit; or, lacking that, an oral message from the Building Clerk about the seeds of trouble that the granting of any particular application might sow.

Another forty percent of the matters before the Huntington Board involved hearings of an adversarial nature which, like the nonadversarial ones, we mention just in passing. They did involve confrontations between homeowners and their neighbors, because the applicants wanted to do certain things that seemed to their neighbors to be deleterious with respect to their own homes. One of the most common causes of this kind of controversy was a homeowner's wish to vary the minimum side and rear yard requirements of the zoning ordinance for his particular residential zone so that he could build a garage. This might not seem like much of a reason to go to war, but when you seek to eliminate mandated space between two homes in a suburban area beginning to be filled up by people whose conception of the promised land was a place in which they could have their very own home in what they viewed as wide open spaces, as contrasted with the city from which they came, you may be asking for trouble. If one has spent his last plugged nickel on acquiring a home out of the city, one might not want to be reminded that there are actually only so many feet between him and his neighbor. Also, looking down the road, the resale value of one's home was likely to be thought of in terms of his own conception of what would be attractive, a not unreasonable premise on which to consider such matters.

This is not to say that it was only in the newly developed areas that individual homeowners were serious about defending the protection afforded their sense of privacy and their financial investment by the zoning ordinance. In most of the older non-rural established residential areas, the distances between houses were not great, and if someone wanted to add a garage or put an addition on his house, his application to the zoning board for a variance from the side, rear or front yard requirements in his zone might well produce a protest. Moreover, even in a neighborhood, old or new, in which nobody cared if someone wanted to add to or expand the structure-covered portion of his property, because everyone in the immediate area would just as soon do the same thing when he got the money to do so, this sort of application might be opposed. If you had two neighbors who did not like each other, an application to the zoning board by one of them might well stimulate civic righteousness in the other.

———— ◆ ————

Except for those who were advocates of strict zoning enforcement in a literal, rigid way to the point of being idealogues about it, there was general support everywhere for the proposition that achievement of the goals of a zoning ordinance required the variance-granting and use-permission functions and powers of a zoning board of appeals. After all, it was the only sensible way to implement a zoning ordinance. When this type of law first began to be enacted across the country, and even by the time its vogue came into full flower as the perfect solution to the problem of how to insure that existing and new and expanding communities would no longer suffer or continue to suffer from the urban blight of the 19th century and the early 20th century, there was no way of knowing just what would be the impact on all the individual property interests with respect to which a very sizeable measure of control was now going to be exercised by cities, towns and villages through the medium of zoning ordinances. A zoning ordinance is not a self-executing solution for the myriad of zoning problems for which it establishes the law.

A zoning ordinance is a classic example of a law which may result in a benefit for one person and a loss for another as a function of the manner in which the law is implemented. In this respect, a contested proceeding before the zoning board of appeals was very much like a lawsuit in a court. There was always a winner, and there was always a loser.

However, in a critically important respect, decisions of zoning boards of appeal were (as they and decisions of all other governmental agencies, be they federal, state or municipal, still are) quite different from those in court actions.

Upon a court review of one of its decisions, a zoning board of appeals, like any other administrative body, is not normally required to have based its determination upon a preponderance of the evidence. The precise definition of the amount of evidence required to sustain an administrative body's determination has eluded achievement for the better than 100 years during which federal, state and local governmental administrative bodies have accreted to themselves more and more decision-making authority affecting our lives, it having remained beyond a consensus of judges and legal commentators. However, one thing was and is certain. You don't have to have more than fifty per cent of the evidence in order to win. You can't have so little evidence as to render a decision arbitrary or capricious--but, you don't need more than the other side. The requirement is phrased in different ways in different jurisdictions, seemingly indicating different amounts of evidence required; but, whether the standard be referred to as "substantial evidence" or "some evidence", this kind of determination, i.e., a judicial kind of determination made by an administrative body (usually referred to as a quasi-judicial determination, as distinguished from one made initially by a court), will not be overturned on an appeal to the courts simply because the administrative body's decision was not established by a preponderance of the evidence. Also, on an appeal from the decision of an administrative body to a court, the court will not overturn it simply because the court would have decided the matter differently, because the court is not permitted to substitute its judgment for that of the administrative body.

There is another interesting feature of zoning proceedings. Almost all civil court actions i.e., lawsuits between individual parties, whether they be people or corporations, involve evidence as to what one or the other of the parties did or did not do, and testimony as to whether or not certain things alleged in the pleadings in the lawsuit did or did not occur, or did or did not exist--all matters of demonstrable or inferable fact. In proceedings before a zoning board, the main issue would be whether or not a standard, safeguard, condition or consequence would or would not be met, sacrificed, prevented or brought about by a specific proposed variance or use. Accordingly, what a court would be looking at on a review of a zoning board of appeals determination was really nothing more than whether or not there was a reasonable evidentiary basis for a belief that certain things would or would not occur or be avoided or would be effected by a proposed action. Consequently, even if the evidence in support of an application were well controverted by that in opposition, it did not necessarily follow that a court would find the board's decision granting the application to have been unreasonable, because to a large degree, the board was dealing in terms of extrapolation from known facts (usually very few) to what would be and to what would not be, and what would happen and what would not happen in the future.

For example, one of the standards that had to be observed under a zoning ordinance was that a variance from the minimum side, front or rear lot requirement for a given residential zone would not be injurious to the surrounding property. One might well argue that the very act of reducing the space between the closest structure on a house lot and the common property line of an adjoining lot, typically for the purpose of erecting a garage, would be injurious to the value of the neighbors' property, to say nothing of the neighbors' enjoyment of their property in an area in which people are living and to which they have moved because of the greater amount of space between homes in a suburban area than in a city. On the other hand, one could reasonably take the position that in an area where more and more, life was revolving around the use of the automobile, it would be unreasonable not to enable homeowners in a development in which the homes did not have garages on them to be able to house their cars, citing the convenience of the homeowners in general and also the preservation of property values consequent to not having the streets packed with cars. In any event, it would be extremely difficult to prove that the granting of such a variance would prove injurious to the property values in an immediate area, although given the category of any particular residential zone, it might be just as difficult to demonstrate that the granting of such a variance would not have a deleterious effect upon the property interests of adjoining homeowners.

In a zone in which the minimum-area and side lot requirements were such that the addition of a garage would still leave forty feet between the side of a proposed garage and the side lot line of the adjoining homeowner, the visual impact on the space factor might be relatively minimal, even though the adjoining homeowner might justifiably wish to preserve as much space as possible between himself and his neighbor. However, if one were talking about an applicant whose proposed additional structure would leave only two feet between it and the adjoining property owner's line because of the fact that the side lot requirements in that particular residential zone were so much lower to begin with (the higher zones having greater area and side, rear and front lot requirements), then a change for the worse in the aesthetics of the picture would probably seem more obvious--unless, of course, one already had a number of variances granted for precisely the same purpose in the particular area or development.

The fact that in order to be sustained on judicial review, a zoning board's determination did not have to be supported by a preponderance of the credible evidence but only by an amount sufficient to shield it from being evaluated as arbitrary or capricious, when combined with the reality that in large part what a reviewing court would be looking at was what the zoning board could only find in a crystal ball, rendered it very difficult to overturn a zoning board's decision on a factual basis unless the board somehow had overlooked a fatal gap in the evidence required to have been adduced by the successful party.

In the garden variety of matters before the board, i.e., the ninety per cent of the applications in which it was seldom that anyone but one or two closely proximate neighbors of the applicant really felt they were directly and adversely affected by the outcome, neither the township at large nor any discrete portion of it had any difficulty in viewing any particular zoning board of appeals decision with anything but commendable disinterestedness. In zoning matters, as in most human affairs, whether or not it was one's own ox that was being gored was a weighty determinant of whether or not one's blood pressure might be affected by a decision of a zoning board of appeals.

However, there were applications to the Zoning Board of Appeals that involved issues of public policy, an interpretation of the zoning laws and their intendment, and the balancing and protection of the rights of individual homeowners, rights of areas or sub-communities of homeowners, the interests of those who wished to develop land for residential, commercial and industrial uses, the rights and interests and normal aspirations of those who had been doing business and living in the town for many years, and also the ultimate question of just where, when and in what direction the town should go in these matters. All these applications had one thing in common. They could reasonably be viewed as involving important immediate and long-term consequences for either a discrete portion of the town, geographic or occupational, or for the town as a whole. Sometimes, there might be brought into play concerns about, if not fears for the future quality of life in the township. It is true that if one were opposed to an application, no matter that anyone else in the world could care less about it, one would argue that granting the application would be a bad thing, because it would not only set a precedent for the lowering of standards in the neighborhood directly involved, but would undermine the integrity of the zoning ordinance and thereby have a deleterious effect upon the entire township. Yet, there were applications to a zoning board of appeals that actually did arouse the interest of the town or a significant part of it.

In Huntington, such was the Verme application to excavate sand and gravel.

———◆———

Most of Suffolk County sits on nothing but sand and gravel, once you get below the topsoil that covers it. With huge deposits not only on the north shore, but also in between the north and south shores, the county was a limitless resource for these basic building materials for all of Long Island, including the two largest boroughs of New York City, Brooklyn and Queens. Moreover, Long Island Sound provided a direct route for sand barges to go all the way from Suffolk County's north shore to Manhattan and New Jersey, because it connected with the East River and then with Lower New York Bay. At the time of which we speak, the commercial sand pits of consequence were concentrated in the western part of the county, and the Township of Huntington had a number of them.

———◆———

Whether a house is built with a cellar or on a slab, you are going to be calling for the cement mixer. And so, when the post-war dash to build homes started, one of the first businesses that started to prosper was the sand and gravel business. Owners of sand and gravel pits who, before the war, operated the pits only intermittently, since there was no real demand for the product, were now quarrying sand and gravel continuously. The dramatic increase in business for the industry was of real significance for local people who earned their livings in one way or another from sand and gravel. Families that had operated cinder block and cement-mix businesses for decades, just scraping along, were at last making money. This is not to say that most of the people who worked in the industry made a great deal of money. Yet, the industry did furnish employment to a number of people at wages which, for what one would normally think of as un-skilled or semi-skilled labor, were quite attractive.

In short, the post-war building boom, which one was apt to think of in terms of the land speculators, builders and contractors who spearheaded it, and the new residential communities and their inhab-itants, included the sand and gravel business, the prosperity of which was a direct function of the fact and continuance of the boom, and the existence of which was necessary for all the rest of the forego-ing. The first stage of the industry's prosperity resulted from the construction of houses. Next came commercial, and then light and heavy industry construction. As building construction in our county came as close to being a self-generating industry as one could imag-ine, the sand and gravel business shared its continuing prosperity.

There were three main groups of sand pits in the Town of Hun-tington. First, there were the large gougings on the town's shore line. By and large, unless one was at such a digging, or looking at it from out on the water, the main evidence of these operations was that which one could see from all along the shore--the strings of barges being towed by tugboats out on Long Island Sound, the filled ones going westward, the empty ones eastward, their great distance from the shore making them all look like toys; or, closer in, plying North-port Bay and Huntington Bay, on their way to or from the Sound; or, one might see the sand barges lined up for loading at their moorings at Sand City, at the southwesterly tip of Eaton's Neck, out in North-port Bay. The large deposits at Northport, Eaton's Neck and Asha-roken, the narrow corridor which runs northwesterly from the mainland at Northport toward Long Island Sound and widens into the substantial peninsula of Eaton's Neck, had been mined for de-cades by such large exporters of sand and gravel as the Metropolitan Sand and Gravel Corporation, the Steers Corporation and the U.S. Dredging Corporation.

The other sand and gravel pits of consequence were in the area of town known as Melville, at the far southwestern corner of the town. They were quite large--that of Broadhollow Estates was huge--but all of them were in a General Industrial District, in the congenial company of cinder block, transit-mix and asphalt plant operations.

There were also some smaller sand pits being operated throughout the town. George and Armand Verme's seven and one-half acre pit situate in the corner formed by the intersection of Southdown Road and West Shore Road was one of them.

———◆———

Huntington's first zoning ordinance, adopted in 1930, and its successor ordinances provided that property could be used only for the purposes listed for the zoning district in which it lay. Since the excavation of sand and gravel for commercial purposes was not one of the uses specifically permitted in residential zones, it was effectually a prohibited use in all such districts. The Verme sand pit was in a Residence D District. Nonetheless, it operated quite legally.

Since the inception of zoning ordinances in New York State, a sand and gravel pit, unless it was in a zone in which its operation was permitted (typically only in an Industrial zone), could be operated only if it could qualify as a non-conforming use. In zoning matters, a non-conforming use is a land use which is prohibited by a zoning ordinance but which is nonetheless permitted under the ordinance because it has been going on continuously since prior to the adoption of the ordinance. It is permitted, because to terminate the owner's right to continue a use which has been in existence prior to the adoption of the ordinance would constitute an unconstitutional deprivation of property rights. If the use be discontinued, it ceases to be a non-conforming use, and becomes what it would have been had it not antedated the ordinance, viz., a prohibited use. However, the Vermes had been excavating sand and gravel from their pit in the corner formed by the intersection of Southdown Road and West Shore Road continuously since 1927.

In 1952, it having become apparent to the Vermes that the limit of excavatable material in their sand pit would be reached in the next decade, they purchased for future excavation a close-by nine-acre parcel of land, the northerly and westerly boundaries of which, as a sandpit, would be viewed as unacceptably close to the homes of those who by now resided on Preston Street, Rochester Court and the northerly extension of LaRue Drive. Appended is a sketch displaying the elements of the matter.

The residents of the northerly extension of La Rue Drive, Preston Sreet and Rochester Court had seen the nearby existing Verme sand and gravel pit, and knew that it was an operating pit, when they purchased their nearby homes. However, since there wasn't a great deal of the seven and one-half acres parcel left to be excavated by then, they quite correctly had concluded they had no reason to worry about the existing pit expanding to an extent that it would diminish the attractiveness of their new homes. Moreover, they were effectually shielded from the existing sand pit in one direction by distance and trees; and in another, by trees and some nondescript houses.

———————— ◆ ————————

At the February 1, 1955 meeting of the Huntington Town Board, Supervisor Joseph Cermak advised of a proposed new ordinance for the regulation of sand and gravel operations, which was published in the *Long Islander* of February 3rd.[1] On February 14th, at the public hearing on the town's proposed new ordinance, objections were raised by many to the lack of an absolute prohibition of sand and gravel operations in residence districts. One of the drafters of the ordinance explained that it was felt that it went as far as it could with respect sand and gravel operations without inviting constitutional objections. For their part, the Metropolitan Sand and Gravel Corporation and other sand pit operators (including the Verme brothers) objected to the stringency of the ordinance's requirements. The residents of the homes on Preston Street, Rochester Court, and the northerly extension of La Rue Drive had an active interest in the hearing, since the fact of the Vermes' ownership of their nine-acre parcel and their presumed intended use of it had been common knowledge for some time. Their interest was hardly lessened when the Vermes' attorney, after confirming that the Vermes intended to excavate their new property, asked that Residence Districts D and E be eliminated from the coverage of the new ordinance.[2]

The May 26th edition of the *Long Islander* carried The Southdown Community Association's report of its unanimously adopted resolution opposing the grantng of permits for new sand and gravel operations in residential areas, and advising that it was in favor of the proposd ordinance.[3]

The ordinance had been drafted by three notably capable lawyers: Charles T. Matthews, the town attorney; Loren C. Berry, a town councilman and partner in the prominent Manhattan law firm, Dwight, Royall, Koegel and Caskey; and Schulyer Merrit Meyer, a Manhattan lawyer who specialized in zoning law, and acted as special counsel for the town boad and the zoning board of appeals in zoning litigations. A longtime Huntington resident, Mr. Meyer had been the primary draftsman of the town's original 1930 zoning ordinance, and the leading advocate for adoption of a zoning ordinance. They set about rewriting the ordinance to provide a more effective mechanism for protecting residence districts from sand and gravel pits in a consitutionally permissible way. The result of their efforts was an ordinance (published in the *Long Islander* of June 9, 1955) which, because of its stringent yet rationally based provisions anent rehabilitation, but particularly because of its criteria for granting a permit, effactually gave the town the power, within a constitutionally adequate framework of due process, to exclude sand and gravel excavation, if, when and where it chose to do so. For example, it provided that a permit could not be granted unless the Board of Appeals were to find that "the use will not change the established character of the neighborhood or depress the value of other lands generally in such neighborhood,"[4] and that "the circumstances of the location and the terrain are such that conditions and safeguards may feasibly be imposed to assure that the premises will not constitute an 'attractive nuisance' or threat to the safety of children."[5]

At the June 7th public hearing on the redone ordinance, the primary objection to it, by individuals and civic groups, was that it did not expressly prohibit such operations in residential districts. One smaller sandpit operator objected to the redone ordinance, on the ground that it was too restrictive.[6]

———— ◆ ————

Except for a letter to the editor of the *Long Islander* later that month, in which the writer wondered what kind of town passed an ordinance which no one was in favor of and everyone was against at the public meeting which considered the proposal,[7] the matter lay dormant as a public issue until the beginning of 1956, when the Vermes filed their application under the new ordinance.

The public hearing was scheduled for March 16th. Ordinarily, the zoning board of appeals met on the second floor of the town hall, situated across from the old public library and the town's statue of Nathan Hale, as did the town board, in the room which also served as the courtroom for the town's justices of the peace. However, the room couldn't possibly accommodate the number of people who would be sure to show up for the Verme hearing; and so, the public hearing was to be held at the Woodbury Avenue Elementary School, which was located on Woodbury Avenue about a quarter of a mile south of Main Street, at Soundview Avenue.[8]

The first public manifestation of the campaign against the Verme application began with a letter to the editor of the *Long Islander*, in form a copy of a letter sent to the zoning board of appeals, which appeared in the March 1st issue of the weekly. The letter was from one of the residents of a street which abutted the nine-acre parcel, who wished "to register a protest against the mixing of well-planned and attractive residential tracts with sand and gravel operations."[9] Then, under the leadership of Ruth Corcoran, and apparently largely created by Mrs. Corcoran, who lived on Southdown Road, but whose property was not particularly near the nine acres, there came into being a new civic group, "CEASE--Citizens' Efforts Against Sandpit Encroachment". The first press release of CEASE to appear in the *Long Islander* spelled out the grounds of its opposition to the application as enunciated by its chairman (Mrs. Corcoran) at a convocation of eight residential-area civic groups held at the Huntington Methodist Church on Main Street: The operation would constitute an attractive nuisance, and thus endanger children; it would lower property values of nearby residences; it would cause undue traffic hazards on West Shore Road; it would detract from the beauty of the neighborhood; and, it would be inconsistent with plans for the proposed Mill Dam Park. In the part of the press release which was submitted as a quotation from the Chairman, there appeared the initial molding of the issue as a political one: "We are calling on the Town Board and the Zoning Board of Appeals to uphold the zoning laws we now have, in order to protect the rights of our citizens to own homes and to raise their children in comparative peace of mind."[10]

Also in its March 8th edition, the *Long Islander* carried a full-page advertisement by CEASE, the giant-sized title of which called upon the paper's readers to "Protect Our Children", its subtitle urging them to "Stop New Sandpits in Residential Areas", and which called upon them to attend the public hearing on the 16th. It recited three instances of children killed while playing in sand pits or at other excavations (whether in residential areas did not appear) in Nassau and Queens Counties.[11]

On March 9th, CEASE put on a motorcade which started in Huntington village and went up through Huntington Station to Jericho Turnpike, and then down again to the Toaz Junior High School, the building for which still stands at the conjunction of Nassau Road and Spring Street. The demonstration against the Verme application ended with a rally in the school auditorium. The cars in the motorcade were adorned with placards proclaiming "Stop Sandpits in Residential Areas", "Save Our Children", and "Protest at March 16 Hearing at the Woodbury Avenue School". The featured speaker at the rally was Mrs. Corcoran, who called upon "all parents and homeowners" to attend the hearing on the Verme application and voice their objections to a sandpit operation in a residential zone.

The other speaker was a resident of one of the affected streets who voiced his consternation at having purchased his home "in good faith" in a residential zone two years previously, and now being faced with a sandpit 20 feet from his property and 70 feet from his house. He submitted a free-hand drawing of the area (the appended sketch), which accompanied the weekly's account of the motorcade and the rally.[12]

Also in the March 15th issue of the *Long Islander*, there appeared two letters to the editor regarding the Verme application: one from another resident of one of the affected streets, urging the attendance of all in the township to protect their children from the dangers of sandpits by attending the hearing to register their protests;[13] the other, from a resident of the area but not on one of the directly affected streets, who decried what he refered to as Mrs. Corcoran's appeal to emotions, and who, while identifying himself as one who was opposed to the Verme's application because it could not comply with the requirements of the ordinance, agreed with the drafters of the revised ordinance that an absolute prohibition of sand pits in residential zones would not stand a constitutional test.[14]

In the same issue were nine letters to the editor from the pens of children resident in the developments near the new Verme property, ranging in age from four and one-half to eleven years old, which CEASE had thoughtfully submitted on their behalf. The theme of the letters was the danger the new sand pit would pose for small children in the area.[15] Readers of a cynical cast may have raised their eyebrows at the initiative and compositional abilities of the children.

The last item in the day-before-the-zoning-board-hearing edition of the weekly was a presentation of the position of the Vermes by their attorney, James W. Weber: they would comply with the requirements of the ordinance; their property was in a Residence "D" District, the next to lowest residential classification; their operation would not create a danger; and, upon its completion, will have rendered the property more valuable and of more practical use than at present.[16]

———— • ♦ • ————

Long before 8 P.M., the scheduled time for the Verme hearing on March 16th, all the seats in the auditorium of the Woodbury Avenue School had been taken; and people were standing in the rear of the room and in the hallway at its rear.

The sand and gravel ordinance, as did the zoning ordinance in general for other hearings, provided that in addition to publication of a notice of a hearing, a written notice be mailed to the owners of record of properties within two hundred feet of the outside boundaries of the property that was the subject of the hearing. For those who may not have much of a visual feel for "two hundred feet", it may be useful to think of the distance as being two-thirds the length of a football field, i.e., from your own goal line to the thirty-three yard line of the other side--not a great distance. The number of properties within two hundred feet of the Verme property was eight, and so the number of record owners was sixteen, i.e., the eight couples who owned the properties so situated. These, in addition to the Vermes, were the "parties in interest" the ordinance declared were entitled to be heard at such a hearing. The bulk of the audience were the other "citizens" who, under the statute were also entitled to be heard, many of whom came to be heard, either as individuals or as representatives of various area civic groups in the township. Present also were many residents who were either involved in the sand and gravel business in one way or another or whose businesses were related to it.

As we have noted, in half of the hearings before the zoning board of appeals, there were no presentations on behalf of the applicant, because there as no opposition to the application. In most of those in which there was opposition, which is to say those of a non-commercial nature, the presentation of the request was usually nothing more than a description of the request and its necessity for the proponent, and the opposition to it was essentially nothing more than a statement of the fact of opposition based upon an asserted violation of the spirit, if not the letter of the zoning ordinance.

At the other extreme would be the kind of presentation made by someone who was coming before the board on a project involving a great deal of money--for example, a developer seeking variances on lot sizes or dimensions in connection with a proposed subdivision plat, or the developer of a proposed shopping center, the approval of which was required by the zoning board of appeals, which approval had to be based on the fulfilling of certain criteria spelled out in the zoning ordinance. Even on this type of application, the opposition was normally not especially well prepared.

The Verme hearing brought forth presentations organized in a lawyerly way on both sides, each of which had expert witnesses on the issues that were critical to the decision to be made by the board. All the criteria in the new zoning ordinance were covered, re-covered, crisscrossed and generally hashed over in all possible ways by both sides.

Of course, in most zoning board of appeals hearings that are matters of real public interest--and even if they are not--about eighty per cent of the testimony adduced on behalf of the opposition amounts to nothing more than an expression of a position, rather than the presentation of evidence one way or another in connection with the particular issue. The position, of course, is "We Don't Want It!", the reason for which in this case was that the residents of Preston Street, Rochester Court and the northerly extension of La

Rue Drive, who had been looking forward to the day when the existing sand pit would not longer be operating and might be converted to something more consistent with the ambience of their neighborhoods, simply did not want a new and nearer sand pit. In this particular hearing, the ratio of irrelevant presentations to relevant presentations on behalf of the opposition was somewhat better than most--down to about sixty percent--because the opposition had been organized by a lawyer, and of course, he organized the material in terms of the statutory provisions governing such an application. However, as was normal in zoning board of appeals hearings, which, though quasi-judicial in nature are not run like hearings in court actions, the record was filled with what amounted to nothing more or less than stump speeches.

The hearing opened with the town attorney reading a statement from the town board announcing that rehabilitation would be required in the event a permit was granted by the zoning board of appeals, and two letters from the town engineer, in which that official estimated the total amount of material that would be excavated, and stated the amount of performance bond he thought suitable for fencing, top soil and seeding.[17]

Next came the opening remarks of James W. Weber, the attorney for the Vermes. He was not shy. Adverting to the fact that whereas the Vermes had been operating a sand pit since 1927, he observed that many of those in the area opposed to the application were new in town. He complained that "like locusts they descended on the Town of Huntington, and now they object!"[18] The gasps that emerged from some of the audience[19] did not diminish his bellicosity. After asserting that his clients needed to be able to excavate the nine-acre parcel in order to continue in business, he let it be known that "we're sick and tired of going to public hearings and every contractor in this town is sick and tired of going to public hearings," drawing applause from another part of the audience. To individuals and civic groups who were at the hearing to oppose the application and who were from the Centerport and Greenlawn areas of town, he tossed the following olive branch:

> Pursuant to the present ordinance, we have a right to
> excavate our land if we rehabilitate, and we say to

you people in Centerport, and we say to you people in Greenlawn, would it be fair for us to move in on you and start a sand a gravel business? Think that one over![20]

Julius Michaels, a licensed civil engineer, testified with respect to surface water drainage; adaptability of the land to rehabilitation; the sand pit as a threat to the safety of children; undue traffic hazards; and undue vibration, noise or wind blown dust or sand.[21]

Next, Henry Raymore, a landscape architect, and formerly the executive secretary of the town's planning board, conceding that he had always opposed sand and gravel processing operations, contended that the proposed Verme operation was really a rehabilitation project, since excavation of the land would make possible a "more attractive, more valuable and more practical use of the land." He recalled that during his tenure with the planning board, it had not been possible to arrive at a good use for the property in the existing condition of its terrain. In Mr. Raymore's opinion, "the neighborhood will certainly be better off", noting, with admirable understatement, that "this is certainly not the most attractive piece of land in the area."[22]

The last speaker of the evening was Edward Gold, a real estate broker of some twenty-eight years experience who had been active in the township for two decades. It was his professional opinion that since the nine-acre parcel was essentialy nothing but a hillside, the best thing to do with it was to remove most of it so that it could be utilized for "a moderate priced home building project." He noted that within 2,500 feet of the proposed sand and gravel excavation, there was an oil tank farm having a capacity of two million gallons, served by "huge tank trailer trucks." He noted also that nine hundred feet away from the property, the character of the area was such that in February, 1955 the town board had changed its zoning from Residential E to Light Industry.[23] Like Mr. Raymore, Mr.Gold was directing his atten3tion to the neighborhood of West Shore Road, not the neighborhood of La Rue Drive, Preston Street and Rochester Court.

Although the hearing had begun on time, it ended for the evening even before the Vermes had completed their presentation. It wasn't that the presentation on behalf of the Vermes was particularly lengthy, considering the nature of the hearing and the seriousness of the opposition to the application. The reason was that a blizzard was in progress; and around ten o'clock, the lights went out. After waiting for a half hour for them to come on again, Edwin F. Brooks, Chairman of the Zoning Board of Appeals, adjourned the hearing to April 6th.[24]

Circulation of the Welcome Wagon remarks of the Vermes' attorney was not limited to word of mouth by the hundreds of townspeople at the hearing. They were disseminated also by the March 22nd the *Long Islander*, which carried a letter of protest from one of the La Rue Drive record owners, a composition well designed to arouse all others who had come to Huntington following World War II.[25] The letter was a harbinger of 1957, because in form it was a letter to Joseph Cermak, the town's Supervisor. The writer had sent a copy to the editor of the *Long Islander*, with the note, "I thought you might be interested. Thank you." The letter, which called for an apology from the attorney for having "hurt so many of our townspeople" by the words he uttered "in a public place and on public record", was clearly an invitation to the Supervisor to disassociate himself publicly from the sentiments articulated by counsel for the Vermes, notwithstanding that for him to have done this during the pendency of the application would have been clearly improper; and, that for him to do so after the decision would have been highly unlikely, even though it is at least as unlikely that privately he did not curse the lawyer for what he had done.

The *Long Islander* of March 29th exhibited a drawing submitted by CEASE. It showed a man playing a fiddle. The back of his shirt carried the insignia, "Huntington Home Owner". The man was standing at the base of a very high and almost vertical sand embankment, on the top of which was a house that was very close to the edge, over which a tree was falling. To the left of the fiddler was a steam shovel. In the distance was a second mountainous sand bank with another house close to the edge. Finally, to the left of the steam shovel, under the caption, "This may be your child," were two grave diggers and some crosses.[26]

When the hearing resumed on April 6th, the attorney for the Vermes preceded the continuation of his case with an apology to anyone who might have taken offense at his reference to the town's newer residents as locusts. Mr. Weber explained that it had not been his intention to disparage anyone. He added that he did not doubt that all residents had an equal interest in the good of the town. Eventually, he outdid himself. Presumably because the letter published in the *Long Islander* had asserted that his remarks manifested an "intolerance [which] is both unwholesome and outdated and completely inconsistent with the spirit that made our nation great," he even went so far as to state for the record that he had no prejudices referable to race, creed or color. His final words on the subject were, "I apologize with humble sincerity to anyone I may have offended."[27]

An assortment of nine people--friends of the Vermes, West Shore Road residents in the proximity of the existing sand pit, other people in the sand and gravel business, a local home builder, and a nephew of George and Armand Verme (citing a verse in the Bible in support of his uncles), spoke on behalf of the Vermes. The presentation of expert and lay testimony in support of the application was now complete.[28]

The case for the opponents opened with the unveiling of an aerial photograph showing the existing sand pit, the property proposed to be excavated, and the homes within two hundred feet of the latter. Each of the sixteen owners of record of these homes paraded to the microphone and identified his house. In sum, they testified in substance that they had come to Huntington because they thought it was such a nice place to live and bring up their children; that the proposed sand and gravel operation would destroy the character of the neighborhood, lower the value of their homes, pose unacceptable danger for their children by reason of being an attractive nuisance, and the truck traffic the operation would create, all of which would necessitate their removal from the area with an attendant loss of money consequent to the lowered value of their properties.[29]

Their first expert witness was Homer Neville, an agronomist affiliated with the Long Island Agricultural and Technical Institute at Farmingdale, who gave it as his opinion that while stabilization of the slopes created by the proposed excavation would not be unachievable, it would be a formidable task that would take a long, long time to accomplish. Fred J. Biele, a professional engineer of many years practice in the county, pointed out that the rehabilitation could not be started while the excavation was going on, and identified some properties which demonstrated that such rehabilitation was more easily said than done.[30]

The third person testifying as an expert was William R. Donaldson, who brought with him an extensive background in real estate, as a broker, developer, and mortgage appraiser for banks. Mr. Donaldson declared that the character of the neighborhood would be destroyed, with a consequential lowering of its property values for both sale and mortgage purposes. Also, in his opinion, in addition to use of the land for sand and gravel excavation being incompatible with the residential use of the area, its production of vibration, noise and wind blown sand and dust would be most onerous for the residents of the area.[31]

Also speaking in opposition to the application was Raymond O'Pray, President of the Centerport Civic Association, who asserted that it was the obligation of the board of zoning appeals not to allow this kind of operation in a residential zone. The featured speaker in opposition, other than the homeowners within 200 feet and their expert witnesses, was Mrs. Corcoran, who brought with her a petition signed by 2,465 people who were against the proposal, as well as a number of letters expressing displeasure with the prospect of such an activity in a residential area. She explained that CEASE represented sixty-two different organizations having a civic interest in the matter; and, that it spoke for homeowners throughout the township who were appalled at the idea of allowing sand and gravel pit operations in residential districts. In addition to Mrs. Corcoran, there were twenty other speakers in opposition to the application.[32]

Many of the signatures on the petition which Mrs. Corcoran filed with the board were those of railroad commuters. They were obtained by people who plied the railroad stations serving the town-- East Northport, Greenlawn, Huntington and Cold Spring Harbor-- between 5:30 and 8:30 in the morning with information fliers and petition sheets. Some of the residents they approached took sheets with them and obtained signatures themselves in their neighborhoods.[33]

During his summation, Mr. Weber presented a petition signed by 2,325 people in favor of his clients' application.[34] Although his summation, like his adversary's, was short, in deference to the lateness of the hour,[35] he found room in it to point out that unlike the opponents of the application, the Vermes did not have to resort to getting signatures from commuters. Not surprisingly, the next issue of the *Long Islander* carried three letters raking him over the coals for that bit of gratuitous condescension. The first was from one of the record owners, who took the opportunity to make it clear that she, unlike some people, thought commuters were very nice civic-minded people.[36] (If one counted those who commuted to the city by car as well as those who took the Long Island Railroad, commuters constituted a significant portion of the town's wage earners by 1956.) A second letter was from a commuter, who took the occasion to point out that commuters were first class citizens and had just as much right as those who worked in town to voice their opinions, and who praised CEASE for its efforts on behalf of the town's residential areas.[37] The third letter writer was also someone who had signed a petition at a train station. After reprimanding the Vermes' attorney for his derisive reference to commuters, the writer commended the CEASE people for the civic-mindedness manifested by their early morning endeavors.[38]

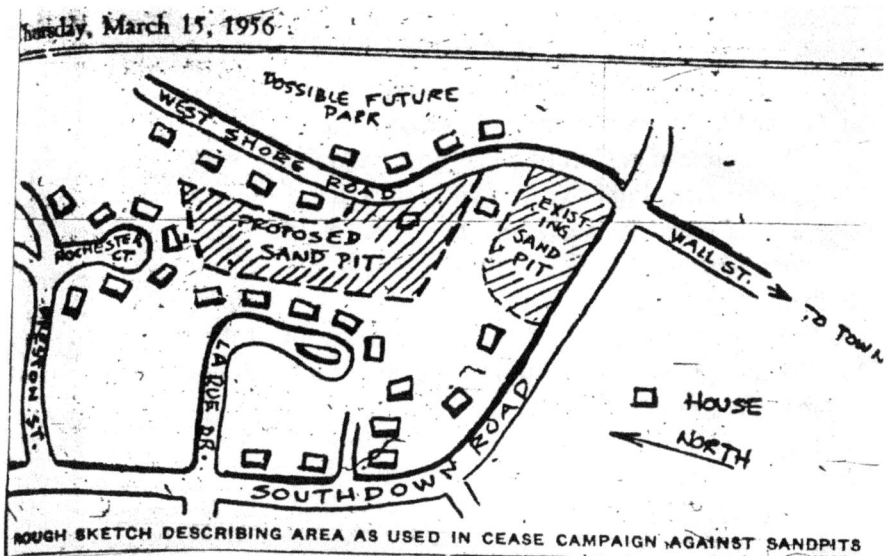

ROUGH SKETCH DESCRIBING AREA AS USED IN CEASE CAMPAIGN AGAINST SANDPITS

Notes

1. "More Sand Control Sought By Town in Proposed Ordinance," *Long Islander*, February 3, 1955.
2. "Proposed Sand and Gravel Ordinance Under Heavy Fire," ibid., February 17, 1955.
3. "Extension of Sand and Gravel Digging Opposed by Civics," ibid., May 26, 1955.
4. Building Zone Ordinance of the Town of Huntington, Section 3 (f).
5. Ibid., Section 3 (c).
6. "Newest Gravel Code Not Srong Enough, Civic Groups State," *Long Islander*, June 9, 1955
7. Daniel W. Bowman, letter to the editor, ibid., June 16, 1955.
8. "Several More Sand, Gravel Pits Are Pending Action," ibid., March 1, 1956.
9. Helen D. Katibah, letter to the editor, ibid.
10. "Civic Groups Oppose Sandpit Extension in Residence Areas," *Long Islander*, March 8, 1956.
11. "Protect Our Children," ibid.
12. "CEASE Motorcade Is Demonstration Against Sandpits," *Long Islander*, March 15, 1956.
13. Lorraine J. Howard, letter to the editor, ibid.
14. Gerard J. Davies, letter to the editor, ibid.
15. "Children Join in Campaign Against Sand Excavation," ibid.
16. "Weber Asks Public to Weigh Facts in Sand Application," ibid.
17. "Gravel Hearing Cut Short by Light Failure; Adjourned," *Long Islander*, March 22, 1956.
18. Ibid.
19. Not noted by the *Long Islander* in its account of the hearing.
20. "Gravel Hearing Cut Short by Light Failure; Adjourned," *Long Islander*, March 22, 1956.
21. Ibid.
22. Ibid.
23. Ibid.
24. Ibid.
25. Kathryn M. Smith, letter to the editor, *Long Islander*, March 22, 1956.

26. Drawing entitled "Stop", ibid., March 29, 1956.
27. "Objectors Voice Fears of Sandpit om Residence District," ibid., April 12, 1956.
28. Ibid.
29. Ibid.
30. Ibid.
31. Ibid.
32. Ibid.
33. See Bernice Reilly, letter to the editor, *Long Islander*, April 12, 1956.
34. "Objectors Voice Fears of Sandpit in Residence Area," ibid.
35. Ibid.
36. Bernice Reilly, letter to the editor, *Long Islander*, April 12, 1956.
37. Dr. Robert C. Ottke, letter to the editor, ibid.
38. Louis Calumet, letter to the editor, ibid.

Chapter 7

John Hulsen was born in Brooklyn in 1898. When he was nine years old, his father, who had been a grocer in the city, moved out to the West Hills section of Huntington, where he became a farmer. In 1912, upon attaining the age of fourteen years, and thus being eligible for working papers, John ended his schooling after only sixteen days in high school. He first went to work as a mule driver on the estate of Ogden Mills, whose son, Ogden L. Mills, would become Under-Secretary of the Treasury under Presidents Coolidge and Hoover, and ultimately Secretary of the Treasury in the last year of the Hoover administration. Subsequently, he entered the employ of the financier, Otto Kahn, on his 500-acre Cold Spring Harbor estate. At age eighteen, he became the foreman for the estate. In 1918, John enlisted in the Army, and saw service as a mechanic with the 250th Aero Squadron in France, where he established a reputation as a boxer. Upon his return to Huntington in 1919, he became Huntington's first motorcycle patrolman.[1]

In 1925, he won election to his first term as one of the town's five constables, and was the leading vote getter of the five successful Republican candidates. In the November 6, 1925 issue of the *Long Islander*, the following notice appeared next to J. M. Johannessen's advertisement extolling the unique attributes of "The New Orthoponic Victrola":

THANKS TO VOTERS
I want to thank all who gave me such loyal support

on Election Day and I hope my services may be such during the next two years, that they will meet the approval of all.

(Signed) JOHN HULSEN[2]

———————◆———————

In those days, and for decades thereafter, the U.S. District Court for the Eastern District of New York sat only in Brooklyn, notwithstanding that the District was comprised of the counties of Richmond (Staten Island), Queens, Nassau and Suffolk as well as Kings (Brooklyn). And so, it was in the federal courthouse in Brooklyn, on April 29, 1926, that John was arraigned on a charge of conspiring to violate the Volstead Act. Also held on $15,000 bail on the charge were Bertram Walker, who, running for re-election as a town constable in 1925, had run second to John; Louis Bogard, a deputy sheriff; Henry Hulsen, John's father; and Bill Weber, John's brother-in-law.[3]

Although the arraignment was reported by the *New York Times* on April 30th, there was no account of it in the *Long Islander* in its issue of the following week. However, in its May 14th edition, there appeared a story captioned, "Local Police Officers Asked to Resign", which began as follows:

> The Huntington Town Board has taken cognizance of the fact that the Federal Grand Jury has returned an indictment against some of the officers of the township, and has passed a resolution requesting the resignation of two of the officers who hold elective positions, while in the third case, that of an appointive position by the board, they advise that unless the resignation is received before May 14, the board will take action.[4]

In 1926, the *Long Islander*'s editorials and other commentaries still were to be found on its front page, with straight news stories beginning on the second page; and on the front page of its May 14th edition, the editor commended the town board for its action:

The Town Board will be upheld by public sentiment in requesting the resignation of the police officers of this town now under indictment upon a charge of bootlegging. The presumptive evidence must have been pretty strong to have resulted in their indictment and while under such an indictment their usefulness as guardians of law and order has gone.[5]

The following week, the *Long Islander* informed its readers that the town board, at an executive session, had heard John and Bill Weber present their requests for a suspension of judgment on the part of the board pending the outcome of their trial.[6]

The charge against John's father was dismissed before trial. Bill Weber's trial was severed from the others and put off, because he had sustained injuries in an automobile following the arraignment.

The trial of John, Bert and Louis took place on December 29, 30 and 31, 1926. According to the government's witnesses, which included two Revenue agents, the trio had demanded $2,500 from Paul and Louis Simone as the price for not arresting them for selling bootlegged liquor; they had taken fifteen kegs of Scotch malt as security for payment of the money; and, to add insult to injury, when they returned one of the kegs after having received a down payment of $400, the contents were found to have been watered down.[7] After three hours of deliberation, the jury returned a verdict of not guilty.[8]

Both the *Times* and the *Long Islander*, in their accounts of the acquittals, refer to John and Bert as constables; and nothing in his subsequent public history suggests that John Hulsen ever did anything he would rather not do simply because of other peoples' opinions of him. Accordingly, it is unlikely that he resigned as a constable pending the outcome of his trial. In any event, he was again a successful candidate for constable in 1927, when he again received more votes than any of the other four victorious (Republican) constable candidates.[9] He did not run for reelection in 1929--probably because of another police-work job in hand or in the offing. In a news story in its August 15, 1930 issue, the *Long Islander* reported that Special Constable Hulsen had served a notice in connection with the first enforcement action taken under the town's two week-old zoning ordinance.[10]

———— ◆ ————

Two weeks later, the *Long Islander* carried a front page feature article entitled "Special Officer Hulsen Seriously Burned in Mysterious Accident", and in which the writer refers to him in the opening paragraph as Deputy Sheriff John Hulsen.

A subcaption for the story read as follows: "Persistent Rumors of Gangland's Vengeance, Acid Throwers and Booze Ring Set To Rest-- Statement of Injured Man Explains All." It appeared that John and his friend, John Mullen, had stopped at Bertram's Garage on Jericho Turnpike for gas. The gas tank for the car was situated over the motor; and when some gasoline overflowed, it entered the hollows in which the spark plugs sat. John set about wiping the spilled gasoline from the spark plus; and while he was doing this, John Mullen inadvertently stepped on the starter, causing a spark to ignite the gasoline. The resultant flame caught John in the face, causing extensive burns. During an interview the patient held on the lawn of Huntington Hospital, he assured one and all that notwithstanding that his face, including his eyes, was covered with a cloth soaked in salve, it was not true that he was in danger of losing the sight in one of his eyes.

The story, apart from indicating what John was doing for a living in 1930, evidences the regard in which he was held at the time; and, that the regard was a personal one. After referring to him as Deputy Sheriff John Hulsen in the opening paragraph, the writer referred to him simply as "Johnny" in the second paragraph. The account notes that so many people showed up at Huntington Hospital that Doctor Patiky had to limit his visitors to immediate family. The quoted subcaption is testimony to the fact that he was viewed as a police officer who had taken his responsibilities seriously. The article in its entirety reminds one that in 1930, Huntington was still a small town.[11]

———— ◆ ————

John was first elected Chairman of the Republican Committee of the Town of Huntington in 1943, the victorious candidate of the faction backed by Kingsland W. Macy, the Republican County Chairman, in an intra-party contest,[12] when the Democratic Party in the township was essentially moribund, and the only political warfare of interest was intramural. Everyone on the Republican town ticket won that year, and in 1945, John was unanimously re-elected town leader.[13]

———————— • ◆ ————————

In 1946, Suffolk County was part of the Second Judicial District, which was then comprised of Suffolk, Nassau, Queens, Kings and Richmond Counties. In the absence of a bipartisan nomination, a Republican candidate for a Justice of the Supreme Court seat allocated to Suffolk County normally could not win, since the Republican pluralities from relatively sparsely inhabited Suffolk and Nassau Counties, though substantial for those counties, could not overcome the overwhelming Democratic plurality from heavily populated Brooklyn. However, the 1946 general election was as richly rewarding for the Republicans in the Second Judicial District as it was for the party nationwide, and County Judge L. Barron Hill captured the Supreme Court seat newly created for Suffolk County.

The only fly in the ointment for the newly elevated Supreme Court Justice was that W. Kingsland Macy, the Suffolk County Republican Leader, decided to reward John for his loyal labors and acknowledge his party position of town leader by having Justice Hill appoint John as his law secretary. This was somewhat of an imposition on Justice Hill, since with a non-lawyer in the position, he had no working law clerk. King Macy did this not because he didn't know any better or because county leaders in Suffolk county had a tradition of using the legal secretary position as a sinecure. The appointment of a law secretary was always a political selection, but the job itself was a working position. D. Ormonde Ritchie, who succeeded Barron Hill as County Judge, had served as the law man for the late Supreme Court Justice George Furman. The leader did it simply because that's what he wanted to do to reward a town leader of a populous town who was very good at keeping the troops in line. It was assumed that the matter of Justice Hill's law assistant work was taken care of in some other logistically and politically satisfactory way.

———— ◆ ————

In 1947, in the first week of August, John was re-elected chairman of the town committee for the second time by a unanimous vote.[14]

In November, 1947, following our usual mop-up for our town candidates, and our outstanding vote for our county-wide nominees, John started the practice of expressing in public his approval or disapproval of actions of the town board. This first time out, in a statement for the *Long Islander*, he gave the board a high grade for courage in doing the right thing in adopting a budget increase in an election year.[15] Since the town board had been all-Republican since the election of 1935, as well as since John's first election as leader in 1943, and since anyone who knew anything knew that John exercised complete control over the Republican town committee, what John was doing in public was announcing to the public that the people he put in office were doing what he wanted them to do. Hubris, like love and all the other things in life that are free, can come to anyone.

In 1949 and 1951, John was reelected town leader without a dissenting vote,[16] though 1951 did bring to public notice again for the first time in twenty five years his brush with the law in 1926.

In July, 1951, in the midst of internecine warfare in the Suffolk County Republican organization, at a meeting of the Huntington Republican League, a rump Republican club, Lindsay R. Henry, then District Attorney, made reference to it. According to the *Long Islander* of August 9th, Mr. Henry "recalled that when he was an assistant district attorney he heard of Hulsen's embroilment in a highjacking case being tried in the Federal Court in Brooklyn."[17] At the August 7th meeting of the Huntington Republican Committee, John began his discourse on the matter by stating that Mr. Henry had accused him of hijacking; went on to explain that "high-jacking is robbery", which "is tried in a local court"; and, in the words of the *Long Islander*, advised that "there was not one bit of truth in Henry's statement." He acknowledged that he "was indicted for a violation of the 18th Amendment and the Volstead Act--which means someone in the Town had a 'speak" and Hulsen knew about it."[18] (At the time, it will be recalled, John was on the Huntington police force.)

Granted, the District Attorney's hit-and-run reference to John's 1926 difficulty may not have represented the highest level of political debate. At the same time, while Lindsay Henry's allusion to 1926 was prudently--and for its purpose, necessarily--vague on the facts of an incident twenty-five years in the past, John's response was most revealing about himself in the present in two ways.

First, it demonstrated the kind of mumbo-jumbo explanation that John was willing to use and could get away with by this time when confronted with something that did not reflect well upon him as a public person. He began by setting up a straw man--the accusation that he had committed a crime described as "hijacking"; he then explained for the benefit of his law students that hijacking equals robbery; he then pointed out that robbery is tried in a "local court" (presumably meaning a state court); and then, since Henry's tale referred to a trial in a federal court, triumphantly declaimed the unavoidable truth that no truth inhered in Lindsay's asserted recollection.

The second interesting thing about John's defense was the suggestion that he was indicted because he knew about a speakeasy and didn't do anything about it even though he was a police officer. But, whether or not the government's witnesses were telling the truth in the 1926 trial, there is no question about what John was charged with, and there could have been no question in John's mind about what he had been charged with.

---- ◆ ----

On January 11, 1952 John Hulsen celebrated his fifty-fourth birthday. He had been married, but was divorced, and had no children. However, he did have a nephew, James W. Weber, the son of John's brother-in-law, Bill Weber, who was now serving as an attendant for Supreme Court Justice D. Ormonde Ritchie.

Jimmy Weber was born in Huntington, and grew up there. He had started college before World War II; and then, following his discharge as a Captain in the U.S. Air Corps in 1945, he earned his law degree by attending Brooklyn Law School at night. He graduated in April, 1951, and was admitted to the bar in October, 1951. He was 32 years old, married and the father of two small children.[19] Every young lawyer starting out for himself can use a little help, but at the beginning of 1952, to all appearances there wasn't anything around that John could lay his hands on for his nephew. His own spot with Justice Hill, which should have been filled by a lawyer, would not become available until the following year, when he would be retiring.

But, as we all know, appearances can be deceiving.

Except for three years in military service during World War II, E. Merritt Weidner had been Huntington's town attorney since January, 1938, when the town board, at its first meeting that year, did two things. First, it cut the town attorney's salary in half, from $5,000 to $2,500 per year, because it felt the amount of litigation work had decreased significantly. The second thing it did was to appoint Merritt to succeed Fred Munder, who had won election as District Attorney the preceding fall.

The son of a former Suffolk County under-sheriff, Merritt came from Bellport, graduated from Patchogue High School and then from New York University. His first job was as a teacher in Westbury in Nassau County; his second, chief clerk in the Suffolk County Sheriff's office. He then went to Harvard Law School, graduated in 1934, and came to Huntington, where he went to work in the law office of Baylis, Sanborn and Munder. In the succeeding three years, he worked on town business, appearing frequently before the town board for the town attorney.[20] The appointment as town attorney enabled Merritt to open his own office. During his three years of World War II service, he retained the title of town attorney, while his duties were performed by Schuyler M. Meyer, the primary draftsman of the town's original zoning ordinance in 1930, in the capacity of acting town attorney.[21] From the time Merritt had resumed his duties in September, 1946, he had dealt with the whole gamut of proliferating legal issues that faced the town during the initial period of its post-war expansion.

———— ◆ ————

Since the spring of 1949, the town had been the defendant in multiple taxpayer suits initiated by five residents of Centerport, who had come to be known as "The Centerport Five." The Centerport Five had gone to court to prevent the town from creating parking fields and playgrounds, and from dredging Huntington Harbor and Huntington Bay. The legal action of most importance to these plaintiffs, however, and the first one initiated by them, was that in which they sought to enjoin the town from developing as a public beach a piece of Centerport property it had bought for that purpose.

The town's residents had voted by enormous margins on two occasions for the purchase of the beach property, as part of a program started by the town board in 1944 to obtain public beaches for the town.[22] At that time, the town was in what seemed to the vast preponderance of its residents to be the anomalous position of having forty-eight miles of beachfront and practically none of it available to the public. For public beaches, the town had only Crabmeadow Beach in Northport, Gilsey Beach, a facility of most modest proportions, and a very small beach in Halesite.

In 1950, the town board had unanimously rejected the offer of the Centerport Five to drop all their other suits in exchange for the town abandoning its plans to develop the Centerport beach property as town public beach. In 1951, one of the planks of the Republican town platform had been the continuance of the town's legal efforts to develop the Centerport property as a public beach.

And then, on the Sunday before St. Valentine's Day, 1952, an extraordinary thing happened. John Hulsen, who had no official standing in the town government of Huntington, participated in negotiations, which he had initiated on behalf of the town, with the Centerport Five, at the home of one of them, Mrs. Paul D. Hubscher. The Centerport Five were represented by their attorney and Mrs. Hubscher. John purported to represent the Town of Huntington. He was accompanied by Louis F. Mascaro, of the Huntington Station law firm of Raskin and Mascaro, who attended as Hulsen's personal attorney.

To make matters worse, for some months previously, John had spread the word that Buddy Mascaro was his choice for town attorney when Merritt Weidner's present two-year term expired at the end of 1951.[23] When the town board met in January, 1952, it made all the usual appointments and reappointments except the reappointment of Merritt Weidner for another two-year term. Thereafter, the board informally explained to Merritt that the omission of his reappointment from the proceedings had been an inadvertence. Two days after Hulsen's negotiations with the Centerport Five, with

Buddy Mascaro at his side, the town board unanimously adopted a resolution reappointing Merritt for another two-year term. However, Merritt learned that while the vote, taken in executive session, was unanimous, the board was in fact divided on the question, from which he drew the inescapable inference that it was the division among the board that accounted for his not having been reappointed in January.

And so, what Merritt Weidner was presented with was a quite unauthorized representative of his client entering into negotiations with the attorney for the other side in a lawsuit--an action never criticized by any member of the town board--and being represented in his presumptuous conduct by another attorney. To make matters perfect, Buddy Mascaro was at that time wearing the hair shirt of Democratic Town Leader. There is no question as to what any self-respecting lawyer would have done in Merritt Weidner's position; and there was no question in the mind of John Hulsen, who had known Merritt Weidner since 1935, as to how Merritt would respond to John's blatant provocation. The day after he was reappointed, Merritt tendered his resignation to the Town Clerk.[24]

The *Long Islander*'s request for an explanation of the bizarre bypassing of the town board and its attorney elicited the following response, as reported in the weekly's edition of February 21st:

> Republican Town Leader John Hulsen told The Long Islander yesterday that he had asked Louis Mascaro to be his attorney at a meeting with representatives of the Centerport Five two weeks ago, knowing that Mascaro was head of the Township Democratic organization. He said he knew what he was doing at the time and deliberately employed this bipartisan approach to a solution of the town's legal difficulties in order to avoid any later charge that he had acted improperly.
>
> Mr. Hulsen said Mascaro had nothing to do but listen while he (Hulsen) had nothing to do but report to the Town Board at the correct time such information as best served the interests of the townspeople. If there were no possibility of settlement, then no

harm would have been done.[25]

The response clearly assumed the propriety of the remarkable usurpation of official governmental authority by the party leader. However, since none of the board ever articulated a view to the contrary, perhaps it would be more accurate to say that their authority was not usurped--his was simply exercised.

After a suitable period of time had passed, the town board appointed not one but two successors to Merritt Weidner. It appointed James W. Weber as Town Attorney and George M. Blaesi as Assistant Town Attorney.[26]

When Merritt Weidner returned from military service in 1946, the resigning acting town attorney, Schuyler Meyer, told the town board he thought that the town attorney's salary, which had risen to $3,500 from the $2,500 Merritt had started out with in 1938, should be raised to $5,000, and should be supplemented by $1,000 per year for expenses. (The Town Attorney operated out of his own law office.)[27]

By the time Merritt resigned, the salary had gone up to $7,000. The new Town Attorney would receive $4,500 per year. The Assistant Town Attorney would receive $2,500 per year.

The Assistant Town Attorney had been admitted to the bar in 1939; and prior to the Second World War, had served on the staff of the general counsel of the Mutual Insurance Company. He had been in law practice in Huntington since 1945, and had been the Assistant Town Attorney under Merritt Weidner for two and one-half years. He possessed the usual kind of civic badges requisite for political position and advancement. He was a member of the Board of Education of School district No. 13; District Chairman of the National Hale Boy Scout District; and a member of the executive board of the Suffolk County Boy Scout Council.

The new town attorney had started practicing law in the office of Raskin and Mascaro in February, 1952.[28]

The Long Islander would observe that in view of the litigations which had plagued the town in recent years, the interest of the town was not served by having as its attorney one who though personally commendable had only been in practice for four months, rather than one having the experience of Mr. Blaesi; and took the position that their appointments should have been reversed. It noted that the fact that Mr. Weber was the Republican Town Leader's nephew only invited additonal criticism of the appointment.[29]

———————— ◆ ————————

On January 11, 1953, John Hulsen celebrated his fifty-fifth birthday.

At the February 24th meeting of the Republican County Committee of Huntington, a motion was made to approve the minutes of the February 19th meeting of the Suffolk County Executive Committee, at which Jimmy Weber was approved as the successor to John Hulsen as law secretary to Supreme Court Justice L. Barron Hill that would exist by virtue of his uncle's retirement on February 28th.[30]

Ordinarily, this sort of thing would not have created the kind of controversy that makes for extended newspaper coverage, even in a local weekly newspaper. Notwithstanding the highly critical editorial of the *Long Islander* on the occasion of Jimmy's appointment as town attorney the preceding May, had it not been for Justice of the Peace William E. Titus, it probably would have carried nothing more than the usual sort of adulatory piece on its front page that it always did about anyone from the town who had been selected for a position-- any position. It would be decades before the *Long Islander* would become a tabloid, and it was not always possible to fill the front page without a picture and short piece about a fiftieth-anniversary couple.

As soon as the motion was seconded, Judge Titus took the floor to speak on the motion. He used the occasion to berate the leader for not having obtained the recommendation of his town committee before presenting Jimmmy's name to the county executive committee. The premise of his attack, *viz.*, that town leaders (or district leaders in a city) poll their constituent committeemen, in an open meeting or otherwise, as a condition precedent to recommending an individual for a piece of political patronage, was silly, and he knew this. Additionally, he asserted that the selection of Weber, *per se*, was not the issue, which, of course, was ridiculous.[31] Yet, Judge Titus could hardly have noted explicitly for the benefit of all present, that Jimmy, who was also present as a committeemen, had been recommended by his uncle for a higher paying job than the one his uncle had previously obtained for him solely because he was his uncle's nephew.

However, he did commit the cardinal sin of reminding a good number of the committeemen of that of which they had no need to be reminded. As reported by the Long Islander, he said, reading from a prepared statement, "I realize that many of us hold public jobs at the whim of our political leadership and I do not condemn any who, because they need food, shelter and clothing, vote in favor of the foregone conclusion. I sympathize with you . . . ."[32]

All the foregoing and more was recounted with relish by the Long Islander. It also recited: "In the ensuing discussion, Mrs. Susan Suydam, of Centerport, asked for a secret ballot, saying that only in this way could the real sentiment of the committee be ascertained. Mr. Hulsen said the rules of the county Committee forbade the secret ballot." The motion was approved by a vote of 52 to 1.[33]

The education of the non-politician Republican voters was continued in the Long Islander of March 19th, which reported the proceedings of the March 17th meeting of the Huntington Village Republican Club. The meeting was to have featured a report by attorney Gordon Sammis, chairman of the Huntington Chamber of Commerce's committee to study the town's need to become a first class town; and Mr. Sammis did make his presentation. However, in the event, the featured performers were Titus and Hulsen.

At the end of the question and answer period following Mr. Sammis' presentation, Judge Titus requested permission to address the meeting. He denied that he wanted to be town leader, which may or may not have been the case. However, among other things not complimentary to John, he pointed out that when John stated at the February 24th meeting of the town committee that the rules of the county committee forbade a secret ballot at committee meetings, he lied.[34]

Our Leader defended against this rather straightforward accusation by asserting initially that all had been well with the town before he had been prevailed upon by former Republican County leader W. Kingsland Macy to convince the Huntington Town Committee to recommend the appointment of Bill Titus to fill a Justice of the Peace vacancy caused by a resignation in January, 1947. The result was that Mr. Titus became a member of the town board, and since that time had caused all the difficulties the town was now facing. He had done this in his own name and through his influence over Walter Fasbender, the town's supervisor since 1944. Our Leader did not bother to explain how two members of the town board could out-vote the other three.[35]

————— ♦ —————

In its edition of July 30, 1953, the *Long Islander* carried two sto-ries about Fusaro's Beach, which lay wthin the incorporated village of Lloyd Harbor.

The first reported a July 23rd meeting of the Trustees of Lloyd Harbor at which Supervisor Fasbender talked about the proposed town beach. The Village Mayor opened the meeting by explaining that it had been called in order that the Trustees might obtain an idea as to how the residents felt about permitting a town beach in the village. He made it clear that notwithstanding that the authority to enact the necessary change in the zoning ordinance resided in the Trustees, i.e., that a formal referendum among the villagers was not required, he, and presumably the Trustees felt that the question was one for the villagers to decide. Most of the questions put to the Su-pervisor as well as most of the statements made by the residents who made declaratory statements on the issue evinced untempered hostility to the very idea of the use of a beach in their village by their non-village townspeople. A poll by secret ballot was taken at the end of the meeting. Out of the 122 village residents present, 27 cast no ballot, 19 voted in favor of the beach; and 76 voted against amending the village zoning ordinance to permit its operation.[36]

The second article recited that the Republican Town Leader had appeared at an executive session of the Huntington Town Board meeting of July 29th for the purpose of instructing the Board as to how to go about getting the residents of Lloyd Harbor to go along with a town beach. The sole source for the story appears to have been the newspaper's interview with John had the day after the meeting. However, it does not appear that anyone on the Town Board ever denied that the Town Leader appeared before it in exec-utive session on a matter of significant public interest involving no is-sue of legally or ethically mandated confidentiality.

The article went on to describe the recommendations Mr.

Hulsen had made to the Board. "'I told the Town Board', he said...."[37]

———◆———

Thirteen of the seventy-two committeemen did vote against John at the organization meeting of the town committee on September 21, 1953.[38] However, a week later, when the committee met in convention, the entire town slate (which now included candidates for the four councilmanic positions that came into being as a result of the town having voted itself into First Class Town status that summer) was nominated without opposition. The candidate for Supervisor was Joseph Cermak, who, after a stint as an assistant building inspector, following his service in the Navy in the Second World War, had won the nomination for town clerk in 1945; and in 1949, he had succeeded to his present job, the higher paying elective office of Superintendent of Highways.[39]

———◆———

The 1951 town election had been a particularly humbling experience for the Democrats. Every Republican candidate for town office won in every election district, with pluralities ranging from two and one-half to one to three to one. This was on top of the fact that the Democrats had not won a town office since 1933--hardly a phenomenon, considering the lopsided ratio of Republican voters to Democratic voters in the town. It was clear that the Democrats could not, in the near future, win a town election--not by themselves. However, it occurred to H. Woodruff Bissell, the new Chairman of the Huntington Township Democratic Committee, that if he could bring about a third line on the ballot, that of an independent non-partisan good government group, which featured Republican non-politicians, it would appeal to what many people suspected was a respectable portion of the vast preponderance of the town's voters who preferred to vote Republican, namely, those who would take advantage of the opportunity to vote against John Hulsen. If such a third line had just some of his candidates on it, he would be making progress.

Mr. Bissell stuck his toe in the water in June, 1953, meeting with a group of not more than two dozen at the Bella Vista restaurant in Centerport. Three of those present were Democrats, but everyone else was of Mr. Bissell's target group, viz., non-organization Republicans with a sprinkling of other self-professedly non-political, good government advocates who gave promise of being useful by coming under the spell of the prospect of the promised land of non-partisan government, and perhaps some spirit-lifting self-aggrandizement along the way.[40] After all, the real reason the ordinary voter cannot fight City Hall is that one can never beat the people who fight for the right to occupy City Hall. In other words, generally, one does not attempt to fight City Hall unless one wishes to take up residence there, officially or by connection.

Mr. Bissell explained to his audience that he was satisfied that the Democratic party was interested in joining up with "a genuine independent movement" for the purpose of fielding "top quality candidates," though the town committee had yet to take a vote on such a course of action. He pointed out that with Huntington having just become a First Class Town, one did not have to be a justice of the peace to be on the town board, since the board would now would be constituted by the Supervisor and four councilmen. Consequently, there should be a larger pool of superior candidates for the board. Unfortunately, the Democratic Party itself could not furnish them. He argued that given the various sectional and townwide grievances known to exist, an independent citizens party in coalition with the Democratic Party, with the right kind of candidates, could make gains for good government.[41]

Indeed, by this time, there were many who had concluded that the town government was in the hands of a group constituted heavily by town and county employees who probably could not have earned a living except in those capacities, and even then only by virtue of having obtained their jobs by reason of political activity; and by others who by no stretch of the imagination could ever be described as anything above the level of nonentities, all of whom were controlled by and who followed the orders of someone who was perceived as never having done an honest day's work. If John Hulsen had been wealthy, and just dabbled in politics for the hell of it or because it was the consuming passion of his life, it would have been a different story. But, since he was not someone who did not have to make a living if he did not want to, he was viewed as a public nuisance. The Town Leader was someone who was thought of as a "nobody" in terms of the values and standards of the middle and upper classes of the town. Since he was viewed as a person of no consequence, the realization that he apparently had been controlling the town board for a number of years, brought home to them by his unmitigated gall in chastising it in public in recent years when it did not obey his wishes, understandably annoyed many. There was a growing distaste for a governmental and political atmosphere that was demeaning for them, and thereby disruptive of their general sense of well being.

The only difference in this regard between the newer residents and the older ones was that whereas with the latter it was a matter of gradually coming to the end of their patience, with the former it was a matter of being surprised and annoyed by the realization that apparently one of the less appealing aspects of the urban life they had left--the political machine--was in place in the bucolic paradise which they had fantasized would be their home. The consequence of this was that although most people, regardless of their party affiliations, or even if they had none, regardless of their political leanings in terms of state or national issues, did not participate in town elections, their attention had been brought to bear upon local elections as something to which they should pay attention.

The newcomers complained that the local politicians--there were none but us in office--were abusing and neglecting them. The older and the monied parts of the community were offended at the idea of personages whom they regarded as no more than mini-people possessing governmental powers that were anything more than ministerial. The business and professional people were finding it insupportable that the town should be in the hands of an arrogant ne'er do well who awarded town offices to those of his servitors he adjudged to be deserving of his favor.

It's all right--or it may be all right--for someone to be a mortician, a dentist, a plumber, or anything else that produces an income, security, and perhaps status for the practitioner of the particular trade. We don't really begrudge them these things, even though as often as not we resent the profit they are making that generates the income that, like our own, is the motivation for their getting up every day and going to work. Politicians, on the other hand, are supposed to be selfless, whether they have the money to be so or not. And so, we tend to look down upon working politicians, i.e., those who earn their income, their security (such as it may be) and possibly, eventually, public status, by mining the quarry of representative democracy in a party-system structure for their personal gain and goals. In short, we tend to look at them as public lampreys. This is probably the reason why we prefer not to see them at all. But, of course, there is another reason why we do not carry the existence of these people around in our consciousness. We are inclined to think of government, when we happen to do so, in terms of its service and policy functions, i.e., the services to which we feel we are entitled by virtue of the taxes we pay and the policies it should pursue in our name. Now, politicians are no different in this regard in their non-political, i.e., non-vocational lives. It's just that in the politician's vocational view of government, it represents his opportunity to achieve the same things that we consider for ourselves to be the normal incidents and rewards of an honest living.

What this all comes down to in the minds of those who earn a living otherwise than as politicians and those non-politicians who don't have to earn a living is that only non-politicians are fit to hold local office. There is something more. The Good Government crowd has another common denominator. They know that they're just a better class of people than the local politicians. "Familiarity breeds contempt" is a maxim which applies most severely to politicians. We know that our town supervisor is a political hack. We assume that our U.S. Senator who graduated from being a town supervisor is not, unless he was the supervisor of our town when we reached adulthood or when we moved there.

Of course, in the world of politics and everything it touches, the non-politician is playing it straight, and the politician is not. If the do-gooders are against government by the politicians, the out party is against the machine. If the outspokenly civic minded are for a zoning master plan to preserve the residential values of the community, the organization out of power is out of patience with what it decries as spot zoning. If the advocates of non-partisan government call for a long-range economic plan for the town as an antidote to an escalating tax rate that has resulted from an incompetent political administration, the politicians who are looking to take over are emphatically in favor of government by non-political experts in public administration. It's the old story of one always being grist for someone else's mill when he is in any area in which he is not the professional, the artisan or the tradesman. Whatever his abilities and worldliness outside the entrance may be, once a person passes through the portals of a gambling casino, it isn't that the proprietors of the casino are going to steal from him--it's just that the mark is playing against the House. In politics, the non-politician is always playing against the House. And the House always wins. Even when you think it hasn't. If you are successful, the House you hated because it was evil incarnate has fallen--but only on hard times. The House you will come to hate because you will come to realize that it is but another offering of the same guild is now in operation.

However, non-partisan activists are not dummies simply because they are grist for the mills of politicians. People of intelligence, education and experience in the world as well as in their own areas of competence do not suddenly become Don Quixotes when attempting to advance the commonweal. History teaches the lesson that eventually, through the tortuous process of civic concern and then indignation that leads to formation of *ad hoc* civic campaigns which lead to politicization of issues which presumably were initially non-politically motivated, which then become part and parcel of actual political campaigns as a result of the perception of politicians that another white horse has ambled into view, the efforts of the non-politicians--like those of the politicians who have used the non-politicians as grist for their professional mills--can have lasting, if not necessarily beneficial consequences.

Moreover, quite apart from the long term, both groups--the big names one collects in order to attract the other people who might go for a non-partisan ticket and the latter group itself--get something quite substantial out of their efforts in the short run, whether or not their independent ticket achieves any electoral victories on election day. At the very least, they have the pleasure and satisfaction of bringing pressure to bear on the party in power.

———— ◆ ————

About a month later came the birth announcement for the United Citizens Party, according to which, presented in the *Long Islander* of July 23rd, it came into being at a meeting of "over 100 voters from all parts of Huntington"; it was "neither a fusion nor a coalition party but one without any political ties"; its purpose was "to actively fight the incumbent political machine"; and its goal was "an open non-partisan peoples' administration, for a long-range zoning and economic plan, and for a thrifty and business-like government."[42]

John Tupper Cole, a recently retired Brigadier General, consented to be the United Citizens Party's candidate for Supervisor,[43] but declined to accept the Democratic nomination because it would have involved the UCP accepting part of the Democratic ticket as its own, asserting that the UCP would "make no deals and incur no political entanglements."[44] Joe Cermak polled 9,870 votes, only 144 more than the total received by the General (6,213) and Henry Schantz, the Democratic candidate (3,513).[45]

While the election results dictated the path the Democrats should be taking, they were also significant as a revelation of how the town Republican organization was viewed by a substantial number of Republicans in the town.

When the votes were in, John admonished the committeemen to be gracious in victory. John's way of being gracious was to address all the Republicans who had voted for General Cole with the following invitation into the tent of the town Republican organization: "Anyone who has a constructive proposal will find that it will be listened to by the Town Council or the Republican County Committee. But, don't wait until just before the election to condemn."[46]

With the crushing of an insurgency in the 1953 primary,[47] and the victory of his Supervisor candidate over the nominee of both the Democratic and United Citizens parties, John's position was now unassailable. He won reelection as chairman by unanimous vote in 1955.[48] In the general election that year, the Democrats made matters even easier than before by choosing as their candidate for Supervisor one Albert M. Levert, an attorney who was unopposed for the title of Township Grinch. He had established a formidable record of opposition to any constructive action by the town board or town trustees which conceivably could be a legitimate subject of a taxpayer's lawsuit, i.e., a legal action brought to restrain the town from expending monies, or to recover monies spent by the town for a project. The highlight of his civic endeavors had been to oppose the spending of public monies on the town's tricentennial celebration in 1953. We probably would have swamped Scrooge too.

Yet, even if they had been able to persuade someone less unappealing to run for Supervisor, the Democrats could not have won without a healthy boost from an essentially Republican vote on an independent line. In 1955, there were still far too few Democratic voters in Huntington to elect a Democrat running only on the Democratic ticket, there was no United Citizens Party, and there was no General Cole or anyone else volunteering to lead the forces of good, clean, non-partisan town government.

By itself, the lack of UCP electoral success in the preceding election probably did not account for this void. After all, by the votes it attracted for General Cole, the UCP had laid bare the reality of serious and substantial disaffection on the part of the Republican voters with their local organization. A major reason was the perennial problem that Goo-Goos (the politician's derisive term for political do-gooders) have, namely, that political action organized on an *ad hoc* basis, as distinguished from the practicing politician's continuous plying of his trade, tends to be short-lived.

All of us have certain kinds of activities that form a continuum over our active adult lives. In one way or another and of one kind or another, we all have family lives, social lives, and even civic lives. In addition to these, and underlying them, is one's business or working or professional life. Now, it is true that for most of us, family and social life are to a great extent subordinated to our working lives, but they certainly run a country mile ahead of civic activity in terms of the continuity of attention they command. For most people, civic activity (i.e., genuine civic endeavors, even when engaged in essentially for one's personal self aggrandizement, such as good government crusades--not the civic activity which is an adjunct to if not an essential component of professional political activity) runs a very poor fourth--maybe a little better, maybe a little worse than Monopoly.

That, of course, is why, except in extremely exacerbated situations and in truly rare instances, the non-professional politician, after having expended a disproportionately high amount of energy, time, and sometimes money, in an ostensibly if not truly *pro bono publico* political effort, over a relatively short period of time, at a level of high intensity, is quite ready to go back to his normal pattern of life, which means that the normal priorities resume their position, which in turn means that civic activity takes its usual last place; and since political activity, for most people, possesses less intrinsic value for the community than other kinds of civic efforts, political activity takes its usual dead last place. In other words, after a relatively short period of time in which he has put a great deal of himself into it, he has had his fill. That's why it isn't very often that even a successful fusion effort lasts any longer than is necessary to substitute the politicians of one party for the politicians of the other party in public office.

———— ◆ ————

On May 25, 1956, seven weeks after the second session of the hearing on the Vermes' application to excavate sand and gravel, the Zoning Board of Appeals granted the application. As was the custom, the written decision did not set forth a rationale for the board's determination. It affirmed all the applicable control provisions of the new ordinance; it was thorough and detailed in its requirements for fencing; it contained an affirmative direction for operations to be conducted only at reasonable hours; and it directed a buffer zone of forty feet, twenty feet more than the minimum required by the ordinance.[49]

The *Long Islander* of July 7th reported the appeal of CEASE for funds to take the Zoning Board of Appeals to court.[50] In the same issue appeared two letters regarding the Board's decision. One of them took issue with the position taken by the drafters of the ordinance that they could not constitutionally enact an absolute prohibition of sand and gravel operations in all residential districts; urged the ouster of the members of the zoning board of appeals, if that were possible; and called for political action against those ultimately responsible for disregarding the interests of homeowners by electing new town officers in 1957.[51] The second letter was a copy of a letter addressed to the incumbent Town Supervisor, Joseph Cermak, the peroration of which was that the writer, though a life long Republican, intended to vote for "any party just so long as it is not the Republican Party."[52]

————— ♦ —————

On August 30th, Ruth Corcoran, now an officer of the Good Government Party, hosted a garden party at her home on Southdown Road for the benefit of the candidacy of George Percy, who attended with Mrs. Percy and Thomas Butcher, Mayor of Westhampton. The functional aspect of the meeting was the distribution of nominating petitions in the Good Government Party's effort to obtain a line on the ballot for George in November. The *Long Islander* quoted George as saying that John Cohalan "was a nice guy, and a fellow whom I like very much," but who "would hardly be in a position to prosecute his political friends."[53]

————— ♦ —————

In November, the Supreme Court would hand down its decision. It would find that the record of the Board's hearing afforded a reasonable basis for the Board's decision; it would note that regardless of how the Court might have decided the issues of fact, it could not substitute its judgment for that of the Board; and, it would affirm the action of the Board.[54]

There had been ample evidence on every factual issue upon which the Board had to make findings. It included a plethora of evidence on the issues of whether the use would change the established character of the neighborhood, and whether the use would depress the value of other lands generally in the neighborhood. Thus, one did not have to be a zoning law expert to figure out that if the Zoning Board of Appeals had decided in favor of those opposed, its decision would have withstood judicial scrutiny also.

It will be recalled that the issue of new sand and gravel operations in residential zones had been a matter of widespread non-partisan public concern during the process of adopting a new ordinance in the previous year. A matter of public concern is by definition a political issue in the non-partisan sense of those words, i.e., an issue of public policy to be debated. However, the judicial affirmance of the Zoning Board of Appeals' decision made certain that the issue would have partisan political consequences. After all, we did own the machinery of the town's government. All the elective officials were ours; five of them constituted the Town Board; and the Town Board filled all the non-elective town positions--including the five constituting the Zoning Board of Appeals. Thus, if one wanted to add the patina of autocratic political-machine domination to one's negative characterization of any action or failure to act on the part of the Town Board, the Zoning Board of Appeals or any other town agency or official, it was there for the application. Could anyone deny that John Hulsen, the Republican Town Leader, owned the Republican town organization, lock, stock and barrel, or the reasonableness of the perception that the Huntington Town Board = Huntington Republican organization = John Hulsen? Moreover, to some of those who had actively opposed the Verme application, and to some of the other townspeople who had no patience with the legal hamstrings that prevented learned counsel from recommending an ordinance that would, without reservation, prohibit sand and gravel operations in residential districts, and who were horrified at the idea of a sand pit being opened in their backyards, there appeared a related equation: Vermes = Jimmy Weber = John Hulsen = Zoning Board of Appeals.

————— ◆ —————

Just before Labor Day, 1957, Mrs. Corcoran announced the formation of the Fusion Economy Party from its temporary headquarters in her home. Mrs. Corcoran stated that the new group was not yet prepared to disclose the names of its officers. However, she was prepared to advise that the FEP would be filing nominating petitions for four Republicans, three Democrats and one independent, the last being Mrs. Corcoran. Its candidate for supervisor would be Ernest W. Johnson, a local builder and former President of the Board of Education of School District 13, an enrolled but previously politically inactive Republican. Mrs. Corcoran, enrolled in neither party, would be a candidate for one of the two four-year councilmanic terms to be voted for; and an organization Democrat would be the candidate for the other. The candidates for the unexpired two-year councilmanic term, town clerk and receiver of taxes would be three other previously politically inactive Republicans. The candidates for Superintendent of Highways and Justice of the Peace would be organization Democrats.[55]

There was no indication from the Democrats' newest town chairman, Lawrence Delaney, as to whether or not he had participated in the formation of the FEP slate. In his statement of approbation, he confined himself to pointing out that "since the Democrats are more interested in good government than politics, it looks with favor on the well qualified candidates."[56]

When the votes were counted, Ernie Johnson had 16,533 of them, and Joe Cermak had almost as many--16,439. The rest of our candidates won, but by greatly reduced margins.[57]

————— ◆ —————

When the Republican committeemen entered the American Legion Hall in Halesite for their first meeting following the election, they saw maps of the town's election districts on the walls. Each district was colored to show which Supervisor candidate won in that district and whether his margin of victory in the district was small, comfortable or large. John articulated the only reasonable inference that could be drawn from this presentation: Not all the committeemen had worked hard enough, either on a year-round basis or during the campaign itself. Clearly, this had enabled the Democrats and the Fusion people to poison the minds of many of the newer residents.

The solution was as obvious as the problem. John had divided the town's election districts into nine areas to be administered by sectional leaders. Those selected were committeemen who over the years had been prominent in the work of the committee, in public office or both. However, to insure their effective leadership of the new program of year-round non-stop campaigning, there would be a town-wide coordinator for the committee. In going through the formality of asking the assembled committeemen for their approval of his choice to exercise the authority and responsibility of this new position, John noted, "Some will say 'Jimmy Weber is your nephew.'"[58]

Notes

1. Colin MacLachlan, "Courage and Adroitness Mark Hulsen's Long Career," *Long Islander*, January 15, 1959.
2. "THANKS TO VOTERS," ibid., November 6, 1925.
3. "Constables Held in Bail," *New York Times*, April 30, 1926.
4. "Local Police Officers Asked to Resign," *Long Islander*, May 14, 1926.
5. "Town Board Acts Wisely," ibid.
6. "Town Board Wants to Treat All Fairly," ibid., May 21, 1926.
7. "Three on Trial for Bribes," *New York Times*, December 30, 1926.
8. "Cleared in Dry Conspiracy," ibid., January 1, 1927; and "Huntington Officers Acquitted Last Friday, *Long Islander*, January 7, 1927.
9. "Huntington Town Vote," *Long Islander*, November 11, 1927.
10. "Enforcing Zoning Ordinance," ibid., August 15, 1930.
11. "Special Officer Hulsen Seriously Burned in Mysterious Accident," ibid., August 29, 1930.
12. "Republicans To Name Fall Slate Monday Evening, Greenlawn," ibid., August 19, 1943.
13. "Hulsen Re-elected as Town Committee Head Unanimously," ibid., August 2, 1945.
14. "Hulsen Re-elected Republican Head; Convention Set," ibid., August 7, 1947.
15. "Hulsen Commends Board for Courage," ibid., November 6, 1947.
16. "Robert J. McNulty Likely Nominee for Town Clerk," ibid., September 15, 1949; and "Republican Town Convention Tuesday; Hulsen Again Leader," ibid., August 30, 1951.
17. Bob Rafferty, "Levert Surprises Republicans, Attends Committee Meeting," ibid., August 9, 1951.
18. Ibid.
19. "Weber Is Appointed Town Counsel with Blaesi Assistant," *Long Islander*, May 22, 1952.
20. "E. Merrit Weidner Appointed by Board as Town Counsel," ibid., January 7, 1938.
21. "Weidner Resigns as Counsel for Township," subtitle: "Toaz, Buck and Root Associate Counsel Serves Notice Too," ibid., February 14, 1952.

22. "Fasbender Refuses Any Compromise on Centerport Beach," ibid., February 21, 1952.
23. "Weidner Resigns as Counsel for Township," subtitle: "Hulsen, Mascaro in Negotiatins to End Litigation," ibid., February 14, 1952.
24. "Weidner Resigns as Counsel for Township," subtitle: "Toaz, Buck and Root Associate Counsel Serves Notice Too," ibid.
25. "Fasbender Refuses Any Compromise on Centerport Beach," ibid., February 21, 1952.
26. "Weber Is Appointed Town Counsel With Blaesi Assistant," ibid., May 22, 1952."
27. "Weidner Returns As Town Counsel; May Get Salary Boost," ibid., September 26, 1946.
28. "Weber Is Appointed Town Counsel With Blaesi Assistant," ibid., May 22, 1952."
29. Editorial, "A Political Choice," ibid., May 29, 1952.
30. Republicans Endorse Wickersham For U.S. Attorney," ibid., February 26, 1953.
31. "Titus Challenge To Hulsen Leadership Turned Back 52-1," ibid.
32. Ibid.
33. Ibid.
34. "Hulsen Blames Fasbender, Titus For Town Litigation in Republican Club Speech," ibid., March 19, 1953.
    In its coverage of the June 16, 1953 meeting of the township Republican Committee, the Long Islander would report that John advised that the Executive Committee of the Suffolk County Republican Committee had determined that "the secret ballot at committee meetings would be retained...." (Ibid., June 18, 1953).
35. "Hulsen Blames Fasbender, Titus For Town Litigation in Republican Club Speech," ibid., March 19, 1953.
36. "Lloyd Harbor Turns Down Town Beach; Referendum Next," ibid., July 30, 1953.
37. "Hulsen Proposes Town Share Beach To Get Village Support," ibid.
38. "Hulsen Is Again Choice of G.O.P. in Huntington," ibid., September 24, 1953.
39. "Harmony Marks G.O.P. Convention; Cermak Heads Slate," ibid., October 1, 1953.

40. "Bissell Appeals for Non-Partisan Help in Township," ibid., June 25, 1953.
41. Ibid.
42. "United Citizens Party Organized to Capture Election," *Long Islander*, July 23, 1953.
43. "United Citizens Party Nominates General J. T. Cole," ibid., September 17, 1953.
44. "Gen. Cole Refuses Nomination By Democratic Party," ibid., October 1, 1953.
45. "Republican Ticket Wins All Town Offices, U.C.P Candidates Make Strong Try," ibid., November 5, 1953.
46. "Cermak Believes Party Has Mandate to Do Job Pledged," ibid., Noveber 5, 1953.
47. "Voters Assure Hulsen Leadership of Town G.O.P; Fasbender is Defeated," ibid., September 17, 1953.
48. "Town Committee Re-elects Hulsen; Vote Is Unanimous," ibid., September 22, 1955.
49. "Zone Board Votes Approval of Verme Sand and Gravel Permit in Residential Area," ibid., May 31, 1956
50. "CEASE Will Oppose Board of Appeals Decision in Court," ibid., June 7, 1956.
51. William E. Titus, letter to the editor, ibid.
52. Herbert E. Shore, letter to the editor (copy of letter to Joseph Cermak), ibid.
53. "Percy Addresses Good Government Party Gathering," ibid., *Long Islander*, September 6, 1956.
54. "Court Upholds Zone Board Decision on Sandpit Permit." ibid., November 22, 1956.
55. "Fusion Economy Party To Enter Full Ticket In November Election," ibid., August 29, 1957.
56. "Democratic Leaders Favor FEP Slate, Delaney Declares," *Long Islander*, September 5, 1957.
57. "Johnson Defeats Cermak For Supervisor; GOP Wins Other Town Offices," ibid., November 7, 1957.
58. "Hulsen Names Weber Town Co-ordinator For Republicans," ibid., November 14, 1957.

Chapter 8

On November 26th, Mr. Rigney announced that Joseph Cermak, (still) Supervisor of the Town of Huntington; Edwin F. Brooks, Chairman of the Huntington Zoning Board of Appeals, three other members of the Board, and Mary J. N. Walling, Clerk of the Board; Assistant Town Attorney Charles Matthews; Charles P. McFadden, Huntington Town Engineer, and Alfred Hulse, an accountant, had been subpoenaed to appear before the Extraordinary Special and Trial Term grand jury; and, that state police, armed with search warrants issued by Justice Tilzer, had seized unspecified books and records in Huntington, Manhattan, Brooklyn, Queens, and Nassau County.[1] The *New York Times*, reporting a statement by Mr. Rigney for the newspapers on the 25th, advised that Mr. Rigney "said that the moves were part of an inquiry into possible conspiracy, bribery and extortion."[2] The *Long Islander*, citing a November 27th telephone conversation with Mr. Rigney, advised that the special prosecutor "confirmed that he expected to come up with possible charges of bribefy, extortion and conspiracy and other criminal charges." It went on to quote the special prosecutor as stating that the inquiry by the special grand jury included "investigation of the actions of various public officials and other persons having to do with applications submitted either to the Town Board, the Planning Board or the Zoning Board of Appeals." Its report concluded with the intelligence that Mr. Rigney had appealed for anyone with knowledge of a particular matter to make it known to him.[3]

On December 19th, the *Times* reported an announcement by Mr. Rigney that Mr. Cermak, Mr. Brooks, Robert McNulty, Huntington Town Clerk, Alfred Nussbaum, Huntington's Superintendent of Highways, John Hulsen, the Huntington Republican town leader, his nephew, James Weber, referred to as "coordinator of the town's Republican party", and lastly, R. Ford Hughes, had been subpoenaed to appear before the special grand jury. The *Times* reported also that Mr. Rigney's spokesman "said the jurors would hear evidence of political reprisal threats against Huntington Town highway employees, and more testimony regarding alleged 'payoffs' for sand pit operation permits in the town"; and that he had also disclosed that state troopers, with search warrants, had taken records and books from Mr. Weber's home and office. Mr. Rigney's office also revealed that two newspaper men had also been subpoenaed: Ed Smith, a reporter for *Newsday*; and Clarence H. MacLachlan, managing editor of the *Long Islander*. According to Mr. Rigney, as reported by the *Times*, both of these gentlemen had been present at a meeting of the Huntington Republican Town Committee that had been held soon after the election at which Mr. Nussbaum had stated "that there were 'traitors in the highway department' and that he was going to 'get them.'"[4] The newspaper men *had* been present at the meeting; and Al Nussbaum *had* said exactly what they said he said.

The meeting had begun with the usual formalities, following which the Committee dealt with all the matters that had to be dealt with in an open meeting, which didn't take very long, because the ritual ratification of predetermined decisions does not take very long. The signal to go one way or another on a matter was always made by someone who was known to be speaking for the leader or who was equally well known to be habitually in opposition to the leader. If the latter type offered a motion, one merely had to wait to see if the leader's person made a contrary or even slightly different suggestion. All nominations were made in writing, and none ran more than two sentences. The point is, neither ours nor the Democrats' ever took very long, unless there was actually a power struggle going on, which didn't happen every day. None of the committeemen was happy about Joe Cermak having lost; and of course, everyone was appropriately on his toes in private conversation before the meeting, to let everyone else be aware of how shocked, how dismayed he was; and, needless to say, all applauded vigorously the chairman's warning that we would have to wage a much more effective campaign in 1959 than we did in 1957, and his plea that we begin that campaign that evening.

Meetings of the Huntington Town Republican committee, like those of the Huntington Town Democratic Committee, and all town and county committee meetings on both sides, were, because they had to be, public meetings. Consequently, they were conducted and participated in on the very intelligent premise that all sorts of unfriendly or potentially dangerous people were in attendance. The primary potentially dangerous were the representatives of the *Long Islander*, the main weekly paper for the township, and *Newsday*, the daily paper published in Garden City, in Nassau County, the Suffolk edition of which covered our town and county politics, since the newspapers would happily print things that would better have been left unsaid. Even if the press was not present, there were usually present observers and committeemen who regarded themselves as protectors of the public trust and who would go running to the papers with reports of what they perceived to be uncivic statements; and of course, there were always present those committeemen who were basically disaffected from the leadership because they were not part of it, who would just as soon embarrass the leader if they could by transmitting such utterances to the press. For this reason, no organization person in his right mind ever did what Al Nussbaum did, i.e., to say things that anyone on the other side would love to be able to say that one of us said. At the same time, one could sympathize with him.

———————•◆•———————

When Ford Hughes, John Hulsen and Jimmy Weber appeared before the grand jury, each of them was asked to waive immunity from prosecution, and each of them declined to do so. Whereupon, Mr. Rigney issued a statement in which he voiced "surprise" at their actions, asserting that he had "anticipated that they would be eager to appear and to answer the questions which we had intended to put to them." He continued, "Instead, Mr. Hughes and Mr. Hulsen apparently fall into that category of persons described as the first to wave the

American flag but the last to waive immunity."[5]

On January 13, 1958, the special grand jury handed up two indictments against John Hulsen. The first indictment charged him with six counts of extortion, six counts of coercion and one count of conspiracy. The second indictment charged him and Jimmy Weber with one count each of conspiracy, extortion and coercion. The substance of the indictments was that Hulsen by himself had extorted $23,000 from two different sand and gravel operators; and that, in concert with his nephew, had extorted another $5,000 from one of them. The basis for the alleged extortions was asserted to be Hulsen's threat to shut them down by effecting the revocation of their permits to excavate sand and gravel.[6] (None of the indictments involved George and Armand Verme or their sandpits.)

Upon the handing up of the indictments, Mr. Rigney declared that "this is one of the most important cases to come out of the Suffolk County investigations."[7] One could hardly argue with that assessment. After all, there was no way one could suggest that the accusations were much ado about nothing, as one might have been inclined to do in the case of the Justices of the Peace who simply could not resist making diaries out of their court dockets. As for our side, the galling thing was that if John and Jimmy had done what the indictments said they had done, then they had done it after, and then long after it was clear that the Democrats would be looking for anything they could find, to say nothing of actual criminal activity.

The indictments covered the period between August, 1955 and November, 1957.[8]

———•◆•———

On February 3rd, the Appellate Division dismissed the indictments that had been handed up against A. Russell Richards in October, 1956 for accepting bribes and for perjury in connection with his personal finances. The court analyzed the evidence before the special grand jury, and unanimously concluded that it was insufficient to warrant the indictments.[9]

On February 15th, Governor Harriman designated Justice Arthur Markewich to succeed Justice Tilzer as the presiding justice for the Extraordinary Trial and Special Term of the Supreme court and its grand jury, Justice Tilzer having requested that he be returned to his regular duties.[10]

On March 3rd, the Appellate Division threw out the indictment against Babe Freres. Citing Court of Appeals and Appellate Division opinions of some vintage, it concluded that none of the statutes offered in support of the indictment could save it.[11] In its story about the reversal, the *Long Islander* could not resist the temptation to point out that *Freres* was the seventh "scandals" indictment the Appellate Division had "tossed out" in the preceding ten months.[12]

On April 3rd, the Court of Appeals reversed the Appellate Division's dismissal of the indictments against Milford Kirkup.[13] The same day, the Court of Appeals unanimously affirmed the Appellate Division's dismissals of the indictment against Philip Hattemer for willful neglect of duty, and that against his wife for perjury.[14]

———•———

On November 14, 1957, in the little village of Apalachin, situated in upstate Tioga County, a convention of some sixty underworld characters was taking place. Tioga County was sufficiently rural and peaceful and uninhabited so that in the second half of the twentieth century, its district attorney's office consisted of a part-time district attorney and one part-time clerical assistant. Nonetheless, alert police work resulted in the gathering being raided. The fact of the raid, looked at from a rational point of view, was a tribute to law enforcement. However, the fact that the gangsters were able to get together like other citizens was written about as evidence of a lack of crime control, notwithstanding that apart from some contempt proceedings stemming from the refusals of some of the attendees to talk to grand juries, there was no competent evidence to proceed criminally against any of them. Not surprisingly, therefore, the Governor, in his annual message to the legislature in January, 1958, proposed a permanent crime commission, reminding the legislature that in 1953, Governor Dewey's temporary crime commission had proposed the same thing.[15]

The only problem was that the Governor wanted a five-man commission, to be composed in such a way as would insure a 3-2 Democratic control. Having had to deal with the reality of a one-man

Democratic crime commissioner since 1955, we were in no mood to accept a 3-2 Democratic crime commission, and proposed a four-man commission, to be composed in such a way as would guarantee a 2-2 political allocation.[16] The political realities were that the Governor could not with a straight face veto a commission which, though in fact bi-partisan, would be viewed by the public and the press as non-partisan. And so, the Governor capitulated, explaining that he had been assured by the Republicans that they would appoint outstanding persons to the commission.[17] At the end of April, we appointed our outstanding persons, and they appointed their outstanding persons.[18] On May 1st, the new commission started business, and the office of Commissioner of Investigation went out of business. However, these events did not in any way affect the Extraordinary Special and Trial Term of the Supreme Court for the County of Suffolk, which theoretically could go on forever.

On June 5th, John Britting was found guilty of one misdemeanor count of conspiracy to pervert and obstruct justice and the due administration of law; five misdemeanor counts of taking illegal fees; nine felony counts of asking for or receiving bribes; and nine felony counts of taking unlawful fees.[19]

On November 16, 1956, Francis Phillips, the New York City Police Department Inspector who had been indicted for first degree perjury in October, 1956, had moved for an order dismissing the indictment, or, in the alternative for permission to inspect the grand jury minutes. On June 9th, 1958, Justice Tilzer issued his decision dismissing the indictment.[20]

It appears that Phillips, Everett Updike, a New York State Police Inspector, and Frank Casino, an underworld figure with a criminal record going back to 1925 and no known legitimate source of income, had appeared before the Extraordinary Special and Trial Term grand jury in connection with its inquiry into gambling that began in the summer of 1956. Phillips testified on July 16th of that year. During his appearance, Phillips was asked if he knew Updike and Casino, and he acknowledged that he did. He was then asked, "Have you ever been in his (Updike's) company and Frank Casino's, that you can recall?." Phillips answered, "No, Sir." At that point, Phillips was excused.[21]

When Casino first appeared before the grand jury on August 14th, he refused to answer questions. The grand jury voted to commence contempt proceedings against him; whereupon, on August 30th, Casino once again appeared before the grand jury, this time to give testimony. During his examination, Casino testified that he had known Updike and Phillips for ten years and in that time met Phillips perhaps a half dozen times on social occasions. When he was asked if he had ever been in Phillips' company with Updike, he responded that he had, saying that he had done so sometime in July, 1955, having come across them at a restaurant, the name of which he could not remember, and then having sat down at their table and talked with them for about a half hour, when he left the restaurant, leaving Updike and Phillips together at the table.[22]

On October 2, 1956, Inspector Updike appeared. He testified as follows: In the early part of July, 1955, he had arranged to have lunch the following Tuesday with Phillips. On that Tuesday, they met at police headquarters and then went to Luchow's for their lunch. While they were eating, Casino came over to their table and sat down with them. During a conversation between himself and Casino, Phillips left and did not return. Inspector Updike was unable to say how long it was after Casino came over to their table that Inspector Phillips left the restaurant. Inspector Phillips' testimony as to his previous relationship with Casino was also at variance with that of Casino.[23]

Justice Tilzer observed that it was well established that an indictment for perjury could only be based upon the testimony of two witnesses; and, that Casino's criminal background and the fact that he had been indicted by the same grand jury rendered him ineffectual as one of the two necessary witnesses. The Court, noting further that the charge against Phillips was that he had willfully and knowingly testified falsely when he denied any recollection of being in the company of Updike and Casino at the same time, observed that, the differences in the testimony of Casino and Updike aside, Phillips'

> "No" "to the all important question as to whether he had been in the 'company' of Casino and Updike, without any further elucidation as to the meaning the defendant gave to the word "company", was insufficient upon which to base a charge that the defendant's statement was intentionally and deliberately false and not given through inadvertence, error or mistake.[24]

Reviewing the entire record of the proceedings before the grand jury, Justice Tilzer found that it did not "support or even tend to support the charge that defendant's denial of any recollection of the meeting was deliberately false."[25]
He went to say:

> It is worthy of note that the question put to defendant on July 16, 1956, appeared at that time to be innocuous. He was given no indication of its importance nor was any attempt made to prod his recollection. If after the testimony of Updike and Casino . . . the Grand Jury considered defendant's testimony on this point suspect, it was their duty and within their power to recall the defendant for further questioning as to the alleged meeting [statutory citation]. Had they done so, it is entirely possible for defendant's recollection to have been refreshed to the point that he might have admitted the meeting. In such case no indictment could have been found against him [case law citation].[26]

One can only speculate as to whether, when penning this portion of his opinion, Justice Tilzer had in mind--or even knew about-- the item in the *Times* about the Phillips indictment which appeared two days after it was handed up. After reporting that Inspector Phillips had stated that he had asked Mr. Percy to reappear before the grand jury but had waited in vain to be called, the article continued:

> Mr. Percy was asked on Friday, after the indictments had been returned, whether the inspector had asked to appear a second time before the jury and his request had been refused. The prosecutor said he had no comment. He did say that Inspector Phillips might prove to be a cooperative witness as the investigation continued.[27]

Justice Tilzer took the occasion to observe:

> In passing, it is of utmost importance to note that the transformation of Phillips from the role of witness to that of defendant is wholly unexplained by the grand jury minutes. Where such transformation occurs, the reasons motivating the grand jury should be clearly indicated and not left to speculation or conjecture because they unquestionably involve the rights of the witness and a corresponding duty owed by a grand jury and a prosecuting attorney.[28]

———— ♦ ————

On July 16th, John Britting was sentenced to pay a fine of $500 and serve sixty days in the Suffolk County jail on the misdemeanor count of perverting the due administration of the law; a fine of $5,000 and a jail term of 5-10 years on each of three of the nine felony counts of asking for or receiving bribes of which he had been convicted, sentence on the remaining six of those counts being suspended; and a fine of $4,000 and a jail term of 5-10 years on each of three of the nine felony counts of taking unlawful fees, sentence on the remaining six of those counts being suspended. Sentence was suspended on the five misdemeanor counts of taking illegal fees. The six state penitentiary terms were to be served concurrently with each other but consecutively to the 60-day county jail term. Justice Markewich took the occasion to make the first of the stump speeches he would make from the bench. This one was interesting as an articulation of the jurist's conception of the right to a jury trial:

> I feel that this sentence will serve notice for those who will misuse the public trust and compound it by brazenly forcing a lengthy, costly trial.
> I find it a sort of poetic justice that these fines will be applied toward repaying the county for the money it has had to spend in conducting seven weeks of trial.[29]

By the middle of August, it had become apparent that there would be no courtroom space available for the trial of Commissioner Kirkup, scheduled for September. Mr. Rigney announced plans to use a movie theatre which showed films only on weekends for the trial.[30] However, this did not come to pass, because the theatre owners wanted $1,000 per month for the weekday rental, and the county was not about to pay that kind of money. Consequently, on September 8th, when Justice Markewich next held court, he had to do so in the office of the County Clerk, because the regular fall terms of the regular Special and Trial terms of the Supreme Court and the county court had begun, and there was no courtroom available for the Extraordinary Special and Trial Term. No real harm was done to the conduct of the Court's business that day, since the only purpose of the September 8th session was to set a date on which future trial dates would be set. However, it apparently affected Justice Markewich's sensibilities, because the *Times* reported that he was "visibly upset at the continuing lack of a courtroom". He retained his sense of humor however. When he adjourned court that day, he adjourned it to September 17th, "somewhere in Suffolk County."[31]

———◆———

Although the Governorship of New York had not brought W. Averell Harriman the Democratic nomination for the Presidency in 1956, and although he would be sixty-nine years old in 1960, when the lists would open once again, there was no harm in looking ahead to another possibility of success. Basic eligibility for a third try would, of course, involve his winning re-election as Governor, and presumably doing so by a much larger plurality that he was able to achieve in 1954. Unfortunately, he ran into Nelson Rockefeller, another multi-millionaire who wanted to be President. The New York gubernatorial election campaign in 1958 was a classic demonstration of the remarkable similarities between a political campaign in real life and a school election. In a school election, there are no issues that any student with an I.Q. of more than 60 would recognize as such, and the goal is to persuade the other students that your candidate is the most beautiful or handsome, is the peachiest dancer, and has the most drive. That's what we had in Nelson Rockefeller in 1958. In Averell Harriman, the Democrats had the school wallflower.

———— ♦ ————

At 2:30 A.M. on November 19th, Justice Markewich was forced to declare a mistrial in trial of Walter Salomon, one of the real estate operators involved in the tax lien sale operations of John Britting. The jury had been unable to reach a verdict, and there were no sleeping accommodations in Riverhead, because all of the available lodging space there and in the surrounding area was being used by the land buyers who were in town for the county's annual three-day tax lien sale.[32]

———— ♦ ————

On November 25th, the jury found John D. Carter, the Southampton highway foreman, not guilty of the extortion and perjury with which he had been charged. Mr. Carter had been represented by Edward LaFreniere, an extremely competent criminal lawyer of many years experience, who was also celebrated for his habit of tying up the County Court calendars as a consequence of his representing most of the defendants residing in the county jail who were above total indigence but not by much. It is possible that Mr. LaFreniere did not endear himself to Justice Markewich by his demeanor in court, which his friends and most of the rest of the Suffolk County Bar would have been content to describe as insouciant, though a few, including the Suffolk County bench were apt to view as something less than adequately respectful of the bench. It is a certainty that Justice Markewich was not pleased with the good job that Mr. Lafreniere had done, because, upon the verdict of the jury being received and confirmed by the clerk, and prior to his dismissing the jury, he directed the clerk to "strike the names of these jurors from the roll of jurors of this county", and stated, "That is the only comment I will make."[33] The direction to the clerk was meaningless, since a citizen's qualifications as a juror are not affected by his vote as a juror, and, of course, Justice Markewich, who had served for many years as an assistant district attorney, knew this full well. However, the action of the jury gave him an opportunity to make a political statement, as well as a reiteration of his veneration for the jury system and the right of a defendant to avail himself of it, and he did not let it go by.

Back in June, when the jury found John Britting guilty, it also found Albert Glass, one of Britting's real estate partners, guilty on one misdemeanor count of conspiracy and nine felony counts of bribery. On November 26th Justice Markewich, explaining that he would not "flout medical reports", which certified that Glass was under treatment for a heart condition, gave Glass a suspended sentence of eighteen months to three years, and imposed a fine of $30,000. Just to make sure that no one got the idea that he was going soft, however, the Court imposed some special conditions of probation, in addition to the usual ones specified by statute and the unexceptionable one that he was to continue to cooperate with the Attorney General, if Glass wanted to stay out of jail: Glass was to cease conducting business; he was to liquidate all his real estate holdings; and he was to surrender his driver's license.[34]

———— ♦ ————

1959 started off with the beginning of a court battle which was much more important to Democrats as individual politicians than any of the scandals investigations, which was what they were talking about for public consumption, because it involved control of the Suffolk County Democratic organization. If you are in the good graces of the party and are next in line for something, or something better than the position you are presently filling, then somehow, somewhere, no matter what the election returns are, the chances are that you are going to get some political reward. This is true, even if your party is the minority party. Your party may be the minority party in your town or city, but not necessarily in your county, and even if it is the loser in your county, it may be in control of your state, and even if it's not in control of your state, it may be in control in Washington.

In New York State, every county has a board of elections, which handles the mechanics of the filing of petitions for primary elections and independent nominating petitions, the printing of ballots and preparation of voting machines for primary and general elections, the tabulation of votes, and all the other endless mechanical matters that are involved in the preparation for, the conduct of and the certification of results in primary and general elections. Under the State's Election Law, a board of elections has two Commissioners, who are appointed by the county's board of supervisors, but only after and in accordance with the recommendations of the county committees of the two dominant political parties in the county--in other words, there is always one Democratic commissioner and one Republican commissioner.

When the Democrats took over the state administration in 1955, Adrian Mason, the county's Democratic leader, received an appointment as Deputy Motor Vehicle Commissioner, an unprotected but attractively no-show kind of job. Prior to the Rockefeller administration taking over, Mr. Mason managed to get himself locked into a civil service position as executive assistant to the State Building Commission. However, it paid only a couple of thousand dollars more than being a Commissioner of the Board of Elections, and it involved commuting to work in New York City and also some modicum of presence at, if not necessarily a great deal of attention to the job, bothersome themselves and also inconvenient for the conduct of any entrepreneurial enterprise that might come his way. And so, when the Democratic commissioner resigned at the end of 1958, Mr. Mason recommended himself. The Board of Supervisors, which included one Democrat, William Leonard, Supervisor of Riverhead, initially turned down the recommendation by a vote of 9-1, the only affirmative vote being that cast by Ernie Johnson, the Democratic-Fusion Economy Supervisor of Huntington, who had introduced the resolution for the appointment of Mr. Mason. Once the vote was cast, Supervisor Johnson joined the rest of the board, making it unanimous.[35]

Ford Hughes made his contribution to the current Era of Good Feeling among our friends on the other side by issuing a statement in which he declared that he was "opposed to any county chairman holding such an office. The Commissioner of Elections represents all of the people, and any county political chairman would have difficulty doing that, especially during primary elections."[36] The mention of primary elections was not a reference to the necessity for the honest conduct of balloting or counting of the ballots. It was an allusion to the fact that under the Election Law, the initial forum for litigating the adequacy of nominating petitions in primary elections and petitions for independent nominations for most offices is the Board of Elections. It was also delightful balderdash on two counts. First of all, a county leader fully and justifiably expects his Commissioner of Elections to act on the basis of what he perceives to be his county leader's wishes, unless, understandably enough, he himself is involved in an intramural battle with his county leader. Secondly, Ford Hughes was well aware of the reality that a board of elections is rarely anything but a first, though legally necessary step in the litigation of the adequacy of a primary nominating petition or an independent nominating petition, and that the findings of a board are no impediment to a complete relitigation of all the issues in court. No election law professional would ever accept an adverse board of elections decision as final unless the proceeding before the board had revealed an irremediable weakness in his case, or a weighty political consideration had supervened.

When Supervisor Leonard cast his vote, he accompanied it by the assertion that Mr. Mason should "submit a name that is more acceptable to the board."[37] At three subsequent meetings of the Board of Supervisors, Mr. Mason submitted his own name; and upon the occasion of the fourth offering of himself by the county leader, Mr. Leonard presented the name of Arthur M. Weiss, the Democratic town leader of Riverhead for the previous seventeen years, for consideration for the post, and the board appointed Mr. Weiss.[38] Whereupon, one of Mr. Mason's lieutenants, Bill Ahern, the Democratic town leader of Smithtown, represented by George Percy, brought a proceeding in Supreme Court for an order directing the board to revoke Mr. Weiss' appointment and commanding the board to desist from appointing any person Commissioner of Elections as the representative of the Democratic Party of Suffolk County who was not recommended by the county leader. The Republican County Attorney moved for a dismissal of the action on the ground that Mr. Ahern had no standing to bring the action. The motion was denied.[39] The board appealed, and the Appellate Division, 3-2, reversed the order of Special Term, and dismissed the action.[40] Ahern appealed; and now, the Democratic State Committee, represented by Monroe Goldwater and co-counsel, got into the act, nominally as *amicus curiae*, in the interest of Mason. (Mr. Goldwater was the Goldwater of Goldwater and Flynn, the law firm of the late Ed Flynn, the Democratic county leader from the Bronx who had been the political operator and confidant of Franklin Roosevelt starting when the President was still Governor.) Also appearing, nominally as *amicus curiae*, but in the interest of his faction of the party, was Supervisor Leonard, represented by Henry Zaleski, who would become County Attorney following the Republican debacle of 1959, and Reginald C. Smith, an outstanding member of the Suffolk County Bar, as well as the leading Democratic lawyer in the county. The Court of Appeals affirmed the Appellate division's order throwing out the lawsuit, 4-3.[41]

The case was interesting as a legal matter, producing essentially 50-50 divisions of opinion in both appellate courts. It was no different from any other election law case in that it had nothing to do with the function of the public office to which the litigation was referable, in this case the Suffolk County Board of Elections, which was run by Janet Frace, a very nice, soft-spoken lady, firm in her knowledge of what had to be done by the Board. Both Everett McNab, our Commissioner, who had just been reappointed, and Arthur Weiss were really very nice. Every once in a while, if you were at the board looking at petitions, you might run into one of them. Of course, neither of them could get from one end of the building to the other without the help of Mrs. Frace. This is not said in derogation of the ability of either commissioner, evidence of which was the achievement of his position.

———— ♦ ————

Politicians, like all of us generally, focus on what concerns themselves most directly. Thus, when the new year began, the important news for us and our friends on the other side in Suffolk County was that Governor Rockefeller had approved the continuation of the investigations which Commissioner Shapiro had begun in Suffolk County, as well as those in two upstate Republican counties. This was not news in the sense that it was a surprise. The Governor could not very well close down the investigations forthwith, though eventually, he would bring them to a close. Until he was able to accomplish this, there would be sporadic grumbling by some of our people about his perceived lack of backbone. They saw no reason why he should not sacrifice his political career--and the Republican Legislature theirs--in what they fantasized was their own best interest.

------------◆------------

On February 4th, the jury cleared John Hulsen on his indictment for extortion and attempted extortion and coercion.[42]

On March 16th, Mr. Rigney submitted his resignation as special assistant attorney general. In his statement to the press, Mr. Rigney explained that he was resigning because of the "Republican-controlled Legislature's slashing the budget of the investigation by $150,000." Mr. Rigney complained that when he had conferred with the Governor and the Attorney General on February 18th, "they had given me no reason to believe that adequate funds would not be appropriated to enable me to complete the job in Suffolk." The Governor had proposed an appropriation of $250,000, and the Legislature appropriated $100,000. For his part, Attorney General Lefkowitz, in his response to Mr. Rigney, noted that legislative leaders had advised Mr. Rigney that he could apply for more funding if he needed them.[43] On one hand, this was not exactly a blank check, which is what the Democrats would have liked to have had and which they were suggesting they were entitled to; on the other, we were saying that if Mr. Rigney said and could substantiate that more funding was appropriate, he could have it, which was essentially the same arrangement that had been in effect since Mr. Rigney's appointment in January, 1957.

In any event, Mr. Rigney's peroration was in the best tradition of Mr. Shapiro, including as it did:

> Since I feel that the Legislature's action was purely
> political and was taken to hamper and terminate the

investigation, I cannot give it any semblance of approval by continuing in charge.

In my opinion the Legislature has taken this action because I have moved against powerful political figures.

There are unfinished matters of a most serious nature pending before the grand jury upon which my office has been working for several months. In the normal course of events indictments of certain public officials, and perhaps others, could be expected in the foreseeable future.

It now seems certain that much wrongdoing and corruption in Suffolk County will go unpunished.[44]

The portion of Mr. Rigney's remarks that was not reported in the *Times* included the candid statement, "For months past, I have been under pressure from my partners to return to our law firm."[45]

Mr. Rigney recommended his chief assistant, Edwyn Silberling, as his successor, and he was duly appointed by the Attorney General.[46]

——— ♦ ———

On April 21st, John Hulsen and Jimmy Weber were found guilty of attempted extortion, coercion and conspiracy in connection with $5,000 paid to Jimmy by a sand and gravel operator.[47]

On April 29th, John submitted his resignation as town leader.[48]

On May 12th, Freddie Boergesson, who had been indicted on ten felony counts of accepting bribes and ten felony counts of accepting illegal fees, carrying potential aggregate sentences of $100,000 and two hundred years in jail, was permitted to plead guilty to one misdemeanor plea of accepting an unlawful fee, and was given a straight suspended sentence, without probation.[49] What had happened, as everyone knew, was that Freddie, who made a living as an independent title searcher, did some work for the real estate people who were involved with John Britting. His job as Administrative Assistant to the Suffolk County Board of Tax Arrears was also effactually that of a title searcher. The business of the board had to do with tax liens, because tax liens are the result of tax arrears; but the business of the board had nothing to do with the sale by the County Treasurer of tax liens, and could have no effect upon the preferential treatment Deputy county Treasurer John Britting sold to some real estate speculators. In short, everyone knew that the money he had received from these sharpies had been for title searching services actually performed. There was nothing high about the amount of money he received. All property acquired through the purchase of tax liens requires extensive title searching as a prerequisite to highly technical legal proceedings which are necessary if one is to have marketable title to the property. The properties acquired by the smart apples who hooked up with John Britting were agglomerations of numerous smaller parcels, each of which required these services and proceedings. Nonetheless, though the link between the money Freddie earned and the duties he performed for the board was non-existent, there was the theoretical $100,000 and two hundred years starting him in the face. The acceptance of the plea and the straight suspended sentence was a clear admission of the sham nature of the indictments. However, most newspaper readers probably received the disposition of the case as compassion on the part of the prosecutor and the Court; and the net result for them was the free additional publicity given to the "land-grab" activities of John Britting which were referred to in the newspaper stories about the indictments and the disposition of them.

On May 25th, John Hulsen was sentenced to two and one-half to seven and one-half years in state prison on his felony conviction of attempted extortion, and to suspended one-year sentences on his misdemeanor convictions of coercion and conspiracy. Jimmy Weber was given a suspended sentence of one and one-half years in state prison on his felony conviction of attempted extortion, and to three-months in the county jail on each of his misdemeanor convictions of coercion and conspiracy, to be served concurrently.[50]

On May 28th, Walter Salomon. whose trial with John Britting on a separate misdemeanor charge the preceding November had ended in a mistrial because there was no room to put the jurors overnight, was found guilty. He was fined $500 and sentenced to six months in the county jail.[51]

On July 23rd, Lawrence J. Bauer, the New York State Sales Manager for Dugan Brothers, was indicted on six counts of perjury for

denying falsely that he had spoken with
John Hulsen about the possibility of Dugan Brothers having part of
the county's bakery product business, which at that time was handled by General Baking Company, the makers of Bond Bread.[52]

————— ♦ —————

On July 30th, Suffolk County Court Judge Lloyd P. Dodge appeared before the Extraordinary Special and Trial Term grand jury.
According to the information given to the press by Edwyn Silberling,
the grand jury was investigating zoning proceedings in Brookhaven
Township. Prior to becoming a county court judge on January 1,
1958, Lloyd Dodge had been the County Attorney for Suffolk County, having been elevated to that position from that of Assistant
County Attorney upon the death of the previous County Attorney,
Robert Schur, in a car accident. While he had been an assistant county attorney and the county attorney, Judge Dodge had engaged in
private practice as an attorney, as he was permitted to do, and as
was the custom. When Judge Dodge was asked to waive immunity,
he did so with respect to his acts as a county judge (as he was required to do in order to keep his office), but declined to do so with
respect to any activities prior to January 1, 1958. When he claimed
his privilege against self-incrimination in response to a question relating to pre-1958 matters, he was dismissed as a witness.[53]

————— ♦ —————

On August 6th, the Extraordinary Special and Trial Term issued
an indictment charging Howard B. Wakeman, a senior vice president
of the Long Island Lighting Company, and Robert J. McNulty, Town
Clerk of the Town of Huntington, jointly with grand larceny in the
first degree. The indictment charged that in November, 1956, they
"wrongfully and unlawfully stole, took, obtained and withheld from
the possession of the Long Island Lighting Company a sum of money
in excess of $500 with the intent to defraud" the utility. The indict-
ment further charged that the money was stolen "for the use and
benefit of the defendant Robert J. McNulty and one John Hulsen."

Howard Wakeman had gone to work for the Long Island Lighting Company--referred to on Long Island as LILCO--in 1928 as a clerk. In 1958, he had become one of LILCO's two senior vice presidents. Bob McNulty was serving in his tenth year as Town Clerk. He was also a real estate broker,

What the indictment charged, in short, was that Wakeman conspired with McNulty to use $14,700 of LILCO funds as a payoff to John Hulsen for favorable action on an anticipated application to the Huntington Town Board for a zoning change which was necessary for LILCO to use property it intended to purchase for a generator station. The way they did this, according to the indictment, was to pretend that McNulty rendered services as a real estate broker to LILCO, so that LILCO could issue a check to McNulty, who could then make the actual transmission of the payoff to Hulsen.

The special prosecutor asserted that the indictment depicted "another instance of the political pay-off from which neither the small business man nor the giant corporation seems to be safe in Suffolk. The grand jury by this indictment has served notice that this misuse of corporate funds to pay off public officials will not be tolerated." The story about the indictment which appeared in the *Times* stated that the purchase price of the 46.8 acre parcel was $29,000, which would have meant that the commission would have been 50% of the sales price--arguably, if not concededly, a highly unlikely rate for a non-fictitious commission.[54]

———— ◆ ————

On August 10th, the special grand jury handed up a lengthy presentment which dealt with the profitable use to which Albert G. Glass was putting part of the land he had acquired with the help of John Britting. It seems that it was in the roadbed of a proposed extension of the Sunrise Highway east of Patchogue. Glass had picked up the lots in this parcel for approximately $20 per lot (the same price as would have been paid by anyone else who might have had a chance to buy it had not Glass had a partner in John Britting). He was asking the State for $250 per lot. There were 1,400 lots in the roadbed. $230 x 1,400 = $322,000. The presentment recommended that the county repossess all of the 26,000 lots which Glass had been able to purchase through the courtesy of John Britting, a course of action for which there was no legal basis. The presentment also suggested that had it not been for Britting, the State would have been able to acquire the land in question for a nominal amount, disregarding the fact that there was nothing to suggest that the State had ever asked for a hold to be put on the land for its use.[55]

———— • ◆ • ————

On August 27th, indictments were handed up against Kenson D. Merrill, who before his resignation in May, 1958, had been a justice of the peace and member of the Brookhaven Town Board for eighteen years. Essentially, the indictments, which were for conspiracy, and accepting bribes and illegal fees, charged Merrill with accepting money for zoning applications to the town board, of which Merrill was a member, the legal representation on the applications being handled by other persons, through whom Merrill received the money. Carl H. Hoffman, President of the Bellport National Bank and formerly Mayor of the Village of Bellport, was named as a co-conspirator with Merrill in one of the indictments. Arthur J. Calace, Jr., a Brookhaven town Assessor and Mr. Hoffman were named as defendants with Merrill in another.[56] The indictments were referable to hearings before the Brookhaven Town Board on May 31, 1955, August 16, 1955, and November 25, 1955.[57]

On September 30th, Attorney General Lefkowitz advised Mr. Silberling that the Governor would seek no additional funds for the investigation. The special prosecutor asserted that it was "incredible" that the Governor would do such a thing. He complained that he was being "forced out of business with a full brief case." He added, "No special prosecutor prior to this has ever been cut off with trials and investigations pending. This is a cynical disregard by the Governor and legislative leaders of the public interest. This evinces a public-be-damned attitude."[58]

Also on September 30th, the Appellate Division granted the motions of Howard Wakeman and Bob McNulty for examination of the grand jury minutes, and denied their motions for dismissal of the indictment, without prejudice to their renewal, after inspection of the minutes.[59]

On October 8th, Commissioner of Welfare Kirkup was convicted of twenty-one misdemeanor counts of taking county property and conspiracy.[60]

———— ◆ ————

On October 8th, County Judge Lloyd P. Dodge was indicted for conspiracy, taking an unlawful fee, and subornation of perjury. All the crimes were alleged to have been committed in 1955, in connection with property rezoning proceedings before the Brookhaven Town Board. Judge Dodge was named in three indictments. In the first, he and Kenneth Leeds, a well known real estate operator, were charged with one count each of conspiracy, taking an unlawful fee, and subornation of perjury. In the second, he and Tom Keegan, his former law partner, were charged with one count of conspiracy and six counts of subornation of perjury. In the third, Judge Dodge was charged with six counts of subornation of perjury. A fourth indictment charged Tom Keegan with two counts of subornation of perjury.

Upon Judge Dodge's arraignment, Mr. Silberling explained to the press that "[a]lthough he is specifically charged with taking one unlawful fee of $3,000 fee from Leeds, Judge Dodge received stock interest in two housing developments and approximately $70,000 in fees for handling fraudulent downzoning applications for several clients." Mr. Silberling went on to inform the newspapers that the indictments were the result of ten months of investigation of zoning irregularities in the town of Brookhaven. Unfortunately, he added, he himself would not be able to try the cases, because the funds for the scandals investigation would run out by the end of the month. They would be handled by someone else in the Attorney General's office.[61]

The very next day, Judge Dodge announced that he would not preside on the County Court bench during the pendency of the indictments; stated that he was "not guilty of these or any other wrongful acts", and described the indictments as a "culmination of a series of political acts designed to embarrass the Republican party of this county on the eve of an important local election."[62]

———— ◆ ————

On October 13th, Kenson Merrill pleaded guilty to three felony counts of taking bribes and two misdemeanor counts of conspiracy. The same day, Laurence Bauer, the New York Sales Manager for Dugan Brothers, who had been charged with three felony counts and three misdemeanor counts of perjury for lying to the grand jury when he denied that he had discussed getting some of the county's baking business with John Hulsen, was permitted to plead to one misdemeanor count of perjury, and was immediately given a straight suspended sentence.[63]

On October 15th, the Governor, the Attorney General, the State Senate Majority Leader and the Speaker of the Assembly got together and agreed to the issuance of a Certificate of Necessity which would enable additional funds for the continuance of the Special Prosecutor's operations beyond October 31st, when present funding would run out. Mr. Silberling commented, "I do not believe that the Governor in good conscience could have done anything other than continue this probe as it is now constituted." After all, he reminded us, "this is an independent, non-political investigation." As the county Democratic leader, Adrian Mason, noted, "the Governor and the Attorney General, by their about-face in restoring the probe, have agreed with all honest Democrats and Republicans alike in Suffolk County."[64] Noting the recent guilty pleas and "the one jury conviction", Ford Hughes said that he had "no quarrel" with the allocation of additional funding. "However," he added, "we do point to the fact that over the past four years there have been political indictments which had no basis in law or in fact and which the Appellate Division of the State Supreme Court dismissed. It is my earnest hope that Attorney General Lefkowitz will now closely scrutinize the activities of his subordinate, so that the innocent and dedicated public officials will not have to be subjected to defending themselves against indictments which are without legal or factual sufficiency."[65] In other words, Hughes acknowledged that the decision was the Governor's to make, but made it clear that the Governor would be held responsible by the party for whatever untoward results flowed from that decision.

On October 20th, following a lengthy conference among the Attorney General, Robert McCrate, Counsel to the Governor, and Mr. Silberling, the Governor's office announced that Mr. Silberling would be continued in charge of the investigation.[66] On October 22nd, when the Governor announced that another $81,500 had been made available for the continuance of the special investigation, thus extending it to March 31st, the end of the state fiscal year, he explained, "Corruption must be unearthed and vigorously uprooted, irrespective of the party affiliation of the individuals involved." The explanation for the continuance of a special prosecutor was that there was going to be an election for District Attorney in November, and the Governor felt that the investigation "must be completely removed from the area of partisan debate." The Governor made it clear that his action was not intended as a reflection on the ability of the candidates for District Attorney,[67] which presumably was as close as he felt it politically safe to say that he trusted John Cohalan, the Republican District Attorney, who was a candidate to succeed himself, to do an honest job.

On October 26th, Kenson Merrill, who had been automatically disbarred by virtue of his pleas of guilty to felonies, was fined $15,000 and given a prison sentence that was suspended because of his documented heart condition. Also that day, Milford Kirkup was sentenced to ninety days in the county jail. He had taken the stand during his trial; and Justice Markewich drew from the fact of the jury's verdict the conclusion that the jury had found that Commissioner Kirkup had lied. Justice Markewich could not resist prefacing the imposition of sentence with a homily: "A sentence must be imposed for his lying if for no other reason." Alfred Freistadt, the druggist whom Kirkup had befriended, also suffering from a heart condition, was fined $2,500.[68]

Notes

1. "Rigney Opens New Probe Into Township Zoning on Sandpit Operations," *Long Islander*, November 28, 1957; and "Inquiry Summons Suffolk Officials," *New York Times*, November 26, 1957.
2. "Inquiry Summons Suffolk Officials," *New York Times*, November 26, 1957.

3. "Rigney Opens New Probe Into Township Zoning on Sandpit Operations," *Long Islander*, November 28, 1957.

4. "Grand Jury Calls Top Suffolk Aides," *New York Times*, December 19, 1957

5. Byron Porterfield, "Hughes Dismissed By Suffolk Jury," ibid., December 20, 1957; and "Republican Leaders Refuse to Sign Immunity Waivers," *Long Islander*, December 26, 1957.

    Mr. Rigney's characterization of Ford Hughes, John Hulsen and Jimmy Weber reflected the felicitous recollection of his awareness of a skit at the 1931 annual dinner of The Inner Circle, an association of former and present political writers, reporters and legislative correspondents. Its irreverent skits and songs kidding politicians were performed before hundreds of guests, among whom were city, state and national figures of prominence, political and otherwise. By way of commentary on the 1930 declination of New York City Democratic district leaders to waive immunity except with respect to their offical municipal duties, one of the skits opened with a chorus noting that "Tammany Hall, being a patriotic organization, always waived the flag on the 4th of July, but never waived immunity." ("Reporters Satirize Political Leaders," *New York Times*, March 8, 1931.)

6. Byron Porterfield, "Politician Is Held In Suffolk Graft," *New York Times*, January 14, 1958; and "Hulsen and Weber Indicted On 16 Counts by Probe Jury Investigating Sandpits Zoning," *Long Islander*, January 16, 1958.

7. Byron Porterfield, "Politician Is Held In Suffolk Graft," *New York Times*, January 14, 1958

8. ibid.

9. *People v. Richards*, 5 A.D. 2d 827.

10. "Markewich To Sit In Suffolk Inquiry," *New York Times*, February 16, 1958.

11. *People v. Freres*, 5 A.D. 2d 868.

12. "Freres Indictment Is Dismissed By Appellate Judges," *Long Islander*, March 6, 1958.

13. *People v. Kirkup*, 4 N. Y. 2d 209.

14. *People v. Philipp A. Hattemer*, 4 N. Y. 2d 837; and *People v. Miriam Hattemer*, 4 N. Y. 2d 835.

15. Leo Egan, "Harriman Urges Anti-Crime Unit In 1958 Program," *New York Times*, January 9, 1958.

16. Leo Egan, "State G.O.P. Seeks Crime Control Panel To Replace Investigation Unit,"ibid., March 19, 1958.

17. Leo Egan, "Governor To Sign G.O.P.'s Crime Bill," ibid., March 28, 1958.

18. Warren Weaver, Jr., "State Appoints 4 To New Crime Unit," ibid., April 26, 1958

19. "Two Found Guilty In 'Land Grab' Case," ibid., June 6, 1958.

20. *People v. Phillips*, 177 N.Y.S. 2d 804 (Sup. Ct. Suffolk County, 1958) The writer can only speculate as to the reason(s) for the lapse of time between the handing up of the indictment and the issuance of the court's decision. Neither the decision nor the *Times'* report of it ("Ex-Inspector Here Cleared in Suffolk," *New York Times*, June 10, 1958) adverts to the matter.

21. *People v. Phillips*, 177 N.Y.S. 2d 804, 807 (Sup. Ct. Suffolk County, 1958)

22. *Id.*

23. *Id.*

24. *Id.* at 808.

25. *Id.* at 812.

26. *Id.* at 813.

27. Ira Henry Freeman, "City Awaits Data On Suffolk Case," *New York Times*, October 7, 1956.

28. *People v. Phillips*, 177 N.Y.S. 2d 804, 813 (Sup. Ct. Suffolk County, 1958)

29. "5-To-10-Year Term Given to Britting," ibid., July 17, 1958.

30. "L.I. Graft Trials To Use A Theatre," ibid., August 24, 1958.

31. "L.I. Court Lacking, Land Case Put Off," ibid., September 9, 1958.

32. "Suffolk Land Case Halted By Mistrial," ibid., November 20, 1958.

33. "Foreman Cleared In Suffolk Case," ibid., November 26, 1958

34. "$30,000 Fine Levied in L.I. 'Land Grab'," ibid., November 27, 1958.

35. Byron Porterfield, "Suffolk in Fight on Elections Job," ibid., January 3, 1959.

36. Ibid.

37. Ibid.

38. "Election Job Stirs Dispute in Suffolk," *New York Times*, February 17, 1959.
39. *Ahern v. Board of Supervisors of the County of Suffolk*, 194 N.Y.S. 2d 894. (Sup. Ct. Nassau County, 1959).
40. *Ahern v. Board of Supervisors of the County of Suffolk*, 7 App. Div. 2d 538.
41. *Ahern v.Board of Supervisors of the County of Suffolk*, 6 N.Y. 2d, 376.
42. Byron Porterfield, "Suffolk Leader Wins Acquittal," *New York Times*, February 5, 1959.
43. Byron Porterfield, "Chief of Inquiry in Suffolk Quits," ibid., March 17, 1959
44. Ibid.
45. Colin MacLachlan, "Rigney Resigns as Probe Attorney After Budget Cut," *Long Islander*, March 19, 1959.
46. "New Prosecutor Named In Suffolk Investigation," *New York Times*, March 20, 1959.
47. "Hulsen Is Guilty in L.I. Extortion," ibid., April 22, 1959.
48. "G.O.P. Leader Replaced," ibid., April 30, 1959.
49. "L.I. 'Land Grab' Case Ends In Guilty Plea," ibid., May 13, 1959.
50. Byron Porterfield, "Hulsen Gets Term For L.I. Extorion," ibid., May 26, 1959.
51. "2 Guilty In 'Land Grab'," ibid., May 28, 1959.
52. "L.I. Bakery Official Accused of Perjury," ibid., July 24, 1959.
53. "Judge In Suffolk Balks At Inquiry," ibid., July 31, 1959.
54. Byron K. Porterfield, "Suffolk Indicts 2 In Political Deal," ibid., August 7, 1959.
55. "Land Grab Cited By Suffolk Jury," ibid., August 11, 1959.
56. Byron Porterfield, "Suffolk Official Named In Bribery," ibid., August 27, 1959.
57. Decision dated December 15, 1960, p. 5, *New York Department of State v. Kalman Klein, et al.* (Administrative proceeding against the real estate brokers with whom Merrill was involved)
58. "State Stops Funds for Suffolk Inquiry," *New York Times*, October 1, 1959
59. "Jury Minutes Opened," ibid., October 3, 1959.
60. See *People v. Kirkup*, 196 N.Y.S. 2d 147. (Sup. Ct. Nassau County, 1960).

61. Byron Porterfield, "Suffolk Judge, 2 Others Indicted On Conspiracy On '55 Rezoning," *New York Times*, October 9, 1959.
62. "Judge Steps Down After Indictment," ibid., October 10, 1959.
63. "L.I. Aide Admits Accepting Bribes," ibid., October 14, 1959.
64. "Suffolk Inquiry to be Extended," ibid., Ocotber 17, 1959.
65. "Inquiry Is Accepted by Suffolk G. O. P.," ibid., October 19, 1959.
66. "Silberling Kept On in Suffolk Inquiry," ibid., October 21, 1959.
67. "Suffolk Inquiry Gets New Funds," ibid., October 23, 1959.
68. Byron Porterfield, "Ex-Lawyer Fined $15,000 In Suffolk," ibid., October 27, 1959.

Chapter 9

On November 3rd, the Republicans lost control of the Board of Supervisors, going from a majority of 7-3 to a minority of 4-6, and acquired an aggressive Democratic County Executive for the county's new charter form of government.[1]

From a purely professional political point of view, the scandals investigations, with no end yet in sight, had been an unalloyed success. The day after the election, the first sentence of the *New York Times'* editorial on voting results outside New York City marked the success of the other side's effort:

> The sordid history of corruption and political misfeasance that has been undergoing a long process of exposure in Suffolk County, ancient stronghold of Republicanism, was sufficient reason for the voters of eastern Long Island to give control to the Democrats for the first time in more than a quarter of a century.[2]

On one hand, the election returns came as no great surprise. In a way, we had good reason to be relieved. The fact was, they could have been worse--far worse. After all, when what one is fighting is essentially nothing more or less than a frame of mind that may or not exist in the minds of a really indeterminate number of the electorate, one can never really know until all the votes are in at one of those periodic count'em-ups at the polls on Election day just how well or poorly one's side--or the other one--is doing. On the other hand, it was apparent from the election returns not only from the towns constituting the county, i.e., the results of the town office contests in the various towns, but also from the returns for the county-wide offices, that certain realities had to be faced.

As the pattern of the election results emerged on election night, the collective brains of our party, which is to say the emotions of its working politicians, began to fibrillate. This was understandable enough, given the obvious import of the results in terms of the present and prospective fortunes of all concerned.

Everyone was affected in the short or long term, and everyone was subject to the general feeling that the whole world was going to hell in a handbasket. The syllogism of the panic was as follows: "If things don't turn around pretty soon, they're going to get a lot worse. Something's got to be done. If the Leader isn't going to do something about it, then maybe we'd better have a new Leader. Things never should have been allowed to get to this point in the first place." And so, from the bottom of the mass of the working party, for whom the position of election district committeeman was their full political achievement and status, all the way up to those who could be regarded as movers, the persistent question was, "I wonder what's going to happen now?". After all, whether one voiced one's concerns in terms of "The Leadership got us into this," or "There's no reason in the world why the Leadership should have let things come to this pass," or "We'd better get someone in there who can save this thing--if it isn't too late already", on one hand; or who, on the other, expended their energies on trying to analyze the situation, much in the same way that it is so easy for one to do retrospectively, the common denominator underlying all this mental activity was a quite justifiable and deeply felt concern about what had occurred and what the future would hold.

In this regard, of course, our party body politic was, as ever, no different from the body politic in general in that it is more apt to identify a situation it deems offensive with the symptoms rather than the cause. The assumption, in both cases, is apt to be that there is a specific something that could have and therefore should have been done; and correlatively, that there is the same kind of quick fix just lying around--if only there were someone capable and willing to use it. The fact that the quick fix, i.e., the platform of the party or the program for the party, upon any rational analysis invariably turns out to be nothing more than a vigorous assertion of the proposition that "We will do it better because we can and want to do it better", since the specifics of the platform or the program normally amount to nothing more than a judicious selection of whatever actions or courses of action that have not been pursued by the incumbents, does not alter this self-obscured view of reality.

One might think that in the absence of an historically unprofitable relationship between the party and the electorate, or a clear deterioration of what can be demonstrated as a previously satisfactory one, there is really no good way for an insurgent to get rid of an incumbent--unless the incumbent has already started to drool on his 100th birthday. After all, if the insurgent had possessed a combination of political ability and resources greater than the incumbent, then the insurgent would be the incumbent. The incumbent is where he is because he was able to capture the support he needed in order to become leader of whatever unit or area is controlled by him. He did this by reason of his political capability, i.e., his ability to persuade, to combine, and to lead; and he did it at a time of and in conjunction with a visible and objective threat to the political fortunes and incomes of a majority of the organization, who do not control it, but whose support is essential to the election and continuance of the multitudes of leaders of the organization, starting at the broad base and leading up to the apex of the triangle.

However, the fact is, as history shows, that any pretext will do for an intra-party insurgency.

A change for the worse in the affections of the voters is the most *pro bono* pretext and the strongest weapon that can be effectively utilized by those in the organization who either wish to advance by leapfrogging rather than accepting the normal time progression and chances for advancement, and by those who have reached the point in their political lives at which the only way in which they can ever progress is to make room for themselves further up by ridding themselves of the obstacles represented by the present incumbents in the party structure. If one can actually point to a decrease in the party's effectiveness at the polls, then the wolves who have had to be content with eating after the leader of the pack is done really have something to work with. The fact that the leader may have performed quite creditably, actually, given the totality of the situation, is an irrelevancy. Also irrelevant is the fact that the people leading the charge against ineffectual leadership are the people who are nipping at the leader's heels. "It's time for a new, more vigorous, more effective, more responsive leadership" contains within it all that is necessary to evoke the support of those who, rationally or not, have concluded or can be led to conclude that "Something has to be done!" Normally, what is determined to be what has to be done about the situation turns out to be the political analogue of firing the coach of the football team that's had a shockingly bad season or getting rid of the CEO of the corporation which has had a bad year or two, which is to say, let the most visible personification of the lack of success be the scapegoat.

Ford Hughes knew all this. He was well aware of the corollary of these truths: The scent of blood is always preceded by the sense that blood might be drawn. If the insurgent's or insurgents' intuition in any given situation that the time is ripe for throwing the dart is correct, the scent will take care of itself.

And so, on November 6th, following a two-hour meeting of the party's executive committee--the town leaders of each of the county's ten towns + the vice-chairman and treasurer of the county organization, Ford Hughes decided to step down.[3] While he did not say precisely when the 776 committeemen from all the towns would meet to elect a new leader, it was understood that it would be in the next month or so. By November 12th, the fight for the leadership, which, of course, had begun as soon as the returns started coming in on November 3rd, began to be talked about in the newspapers.

The talk was mostly about our Sheriff, Charlie Dominy, and our Congressman, Stuyvesant Wainwright, III.

Sheriff Charles R. Dominy, the only declared candidate for the chairmanship, stated that his leadership would represent the needed "break with the Republican misguided past."[4] Among the well thought out innovations he would effect would be a code of ethics, under which any officeholder who was suspected of wrongdoing would forthwith be suspended without pay, and anyone convicted of any crime would be barred from ever holding any public or party office. The proposal did have the small defect of being idiotic, since it meant that any political or just baseless charge of illegality would effect the suspension of any official that anyone didn't like or wanted to get rid of, and it also meant that you could be barred from public or party office for an act of such obvious moral turpitude as driving your car beyond the registration renewal date--the crime of operating an unregistered vehicle.[5]

However, Charlie's platform had three important virtues. First, it proclaimed to one and all that if things were presently the way Charlie Dominy would have had them be, Lloyd Dodge would not be drawing his salary as a county court judge after having been indicted for accepting unlawful fees, conspiracy and subornation of perjury. Second, it made it clear that if Charlie Dominy had been in charge, Milford Kirkup would not have been on the public payroll from August, 1956, when he was indicted, until October, 1959, when he was convicted. Thirdly, and most important, it put forward in a form simplistic enough for the voters--in this case the politician voters, i.e., the 776 committeemen who constituted the Republican County Committee--the message that if they did not elect him, the non-politician voters would never forgive them, since, after all, the mass of non-politician voters could hardly be expected to realize that Charlie was just one of a number of pols who would like to succeed to Ford Hughes' position.

The Congressman put himself forward as the leader of a group that he said represented a "better element" and would give the party its "desperately needed new look and restoration of respect." The Congressman explained that a "completely new party leadership" was needed. Accordingly, the first person he ruled out for the leadership was Charlie Dominy, who had suffered the party's misguided past in notable silence as he had advanced his career during that dark age.[6]

Hamilton F. Potter, the outgoing (i.e., just defeated) Supervisor of the Town of Smithtown, who also viewed himself as being among the better element, apparently was another person who felt he could live a complete life even if Charlie Dominy did not capture the leadership. Ham suggested that the New York State Code of Ethics be broadened so as to prohibit sheriffs from holding a political county committee chairmanship. Since no one was aware of how, in the short run--i.e., before acquiring other public employment, Charlie would be able to support himself, many thought that the suggestion might have been made with Charlie in mind.[7]

———— ◆ ————

Like the general electorate itself, the mass of voters who elect the leaders in a political organization are quite susceptible to the virus of hysteria. Like the voter at the general election, the working politician who votes for a leader at any particular level is quite likely to vote for one as against the other on the basis of a reason that in retrospect is seen as quite irrational. We all know (particularly those of us who think we understand such matters because we have been to college and can nod our heads and smile smugly because of our comprehension of the profundities of political editorials and the analyses of political columnists) that people vote against things, groups of people, individual people and ideas, and not for the superior or higher principle or sets of principles. We are all aware of the fact that the most effective appeal to any voter is to "turn the rascals out." In terms of political organization voting, "rascals" means "incompetents". (A leader doesn't get turned out simply because he's a rascal, if it's only the people in the organization who know he's a rascal-- after all, if he weren't a rascal, he wouldn't have become the leader in the first place.) If anything, the working-politician voter is even more vulnerable to an appeal to fear, because he can relate to a much more immediate and logical threat to his own livelihood than the voter at a general election.

People of intelligence and some education (but not too much insight) can be forgiven if they poke fun at the herd instinct of masses of voters in national elections, who, they sagely and sadly (but mostly, condescendingly) say, vote on the simplistic basis of one party being the one that will insure peace and the other war, or that one will bring depression and the other prosperity. The reason we have to forgive this quite accurate description of the way we all vote, i.e., this accurate description of the way in which we seem incapable of defending ourselves against being taken advantage of and being imposed upon by the pols, is that if you put any of these people in a working-politician voter situation, they will act in precisely the same way.

If you tell someone whose livelihood is a function of the party's ability and inclination to dispense patronage to him, whether it be a laborer's job in a town highway department or a position as an assistant district attorney, that "if things keep going the way they've been going we're all going to be out of a job," the chances are only fifty-fifty that he will have the emotional capacity to consider your proposition with anything like the dispassionateness with which it should be contemplated. If, at the time you are trying to seduce him into joining your side in your effort to gain for yourself the leadership, you have the inspiration to assure him that he has nothing to fear in the way of reprisal for coming out on your side because the ranks of those who have already perceived the wisdom of joining you are swelling at a rate greater than even you had hoped for, then you have, by reason of combining your individual political manipulative abilities with the eternal Achilles Heel of fear that is the real target in any political campaign, whether it be intramural or waged upon the general public, made of the fifty-fifty probability a distinct odds-on situation in favor of yourself. The person who knows that his livelihood is dependent not only upon the party being in power but also upon his being in favor with whoever is in power in the party is playing against the house when he is trying to defend himself against the promises and threats being made simultaneously by the contestants for the leadership. In other words, even if there is a justification for our generally condescending and patronizing analysis of the way in which other people vote, as the public, the working politician may be forgiven if in the situation we have just described, he appears to be performing without a full complement of mental resources. If we can understand how a politician at state or national level could make a political career out of, and terrorize a whole state's electorate by shrilling the prospect of "Cheap Chinese Labor", then we should be able to understand how a working politician can be flimflammed by a more high-powered on-the-make politician into casting a lot, making a decision, and jeopardizing his own best interests.

As a rational matter, of course, there is no justification for our not understanding such behavior. After all, the working politician in the situation to which we have alluded, just like the voter at the general election, has no choice. Each type of voter is being asked for support in a war to obtain power. In each case, the support is being sought by means of persuading the prospective supporter that his own best interests will be best served by voting against the other side. In each case the voter is threatened as to the consequences for which only he will be responsible if he does not support the seducer. In each case, the prospective supporter is promised either insurance against the holocaust that will eventuate if the other side wins or relief from the present outrageous situation we're in because others (never the particular prospective supporter himself) were so gullible in the past as to permit the entry of the Trojan Horse. No matter what symbol appears on the posters or on the voting machines or paper ballots; no matter whether the political cartoonists use eagles, stars, donkeys, elephants or Liberty Bells, and no matter whether the evil we must and shall prevent or eradicate in carrying on the work of the Lord is The Other Party, The Other Side, Those in Power, Those Who are Leading Us Down the Garden Path, Those Who Have Led Us to Defeat When We Have Followed Them in the Past, Those Who've Created That Mess in Washington, or Those Who Care Only About The Rich, the goal is the same: to get someone with a vote to help God help the proselytizing politician.

——————◆——————

The aspirant for the leadership who wasn't talked about in the newspapers was Arthur Cromarty, a young lawyer who had just been elected Supervisor of the town of Babylon. And on December 9th, it was Arthur Cromarty who captured the prize.[8]

——————◆——————

On December 7th, the Appellate Division affirmed John Britting's conviction, but found that the fines of $5,000 and
the concurrent 5 to 10 year prison terms on each of the three counts of asking for or receiving bribes, and the fines of $4,000 and the concurrent 5 to 10 year prison terms on each of the three counts of illegal taking of fees were excessive. It reduced the $5,000 fines to $2,000 and the $4,000 fines to $1,000, i.e., from $27,000 to

$9,000; and it reduced the effectual prison term of 5-10 years to one of 2½-5 years.[9]

----------◆◆----------

On December 10th the special prosecutor charged LILCO's general counsel and the attorney for Wakeman and McNulty with illegally obtaining a copy of the Wakeman-McNulty grand jury minutes from the Public Service Commission.

The September 30th order of the Appellate Division granting the defendants' motion to inspect the grand jury minutes included the customary direction that a copy of the minutes be delivered to the defendants upon payments of the stenographer's fee. In his statement to the press, the special prosecutor advised that the copy for Mr. Wakeman had not been completed until October 15th and was not picked up from his office until 4:15 in the afternoon of that day for delivery to LILCO's office in Mineola, in Nassau County, the better part of a two hour drive from Riverhead. Thus, the special prosecutor deduced, it would not have been possible for Harris Steinberg, Wakefield's attorney, to have used that copy of the grand jury minutes for a brief dated October 15th that was submitted in support of his renewal of Mr. Wakefield's motion for dismissal of the indictment, which was made upon the basis of the grand jury minutes, because Mr. Steinberg, on October 15th, was vacationing in Rome. However, Mr. Silberling explained, Mr. Steinberg did not need the copy of the minutes that had been prepared for his client, for he already had the use of another copy, namely, through the courtesy of David Kadane, LILCO's General Counsel, a copy of the copy released to LILCO by Justice Markewich on September 1st, Mr. Silberling charged that Mr. Kadane "surreptitiously obtained a copy of the minutes from the Public Service Commission and used it in preparing an affidavit on behalf of Mr. Wakeman." In response, David Kadane issued the following statement:

> A question has been raised as to how the company inspected the minutes of the grand jury. The inspection was made in an entirely proper and legal manner after the Appellate Division had removed any re-

quirement of secrecy.

A copy of the minutes was delivered to the Public Service Commission for the purpose of seeing whether the company had done anything wrong. The commission, thereupon, had a legal duty to permit inspection of the minutes, because the company had to be given the chance to defend itself--which could not be done without seeing the basis for the charges. That is simple fairness.

Any doubt as to the propriety and legality of showing us the minutes was completely dispelled after the Appellate Division ruled that inspection of the minutes should be allowed. This ruling was made before the Public Service Commission made them available.

The prosecutor's office had been pointedly slow in delivering the minutes, and in fact said it might take a month or more. The special prosecutor would not even permit one of the available copies to be read in his office, or a photocopy to be made by the stenographer at our expense--and this was after there was no longer any requirement of secrecy.[10]

No answer was made by the Special Prosecutor to Mr. Kadane's statement.

On December 14th, the Appellate Division unanimously granted the motions to dismiss the indictment. The Special Prosecutor announced that he planned to seek leave to appeal to the Court of Appeals from the decision of the Appellate Division, observing that he did not know what the ground of the decision was, since the Court's memorandum opinion recited no ground for its dismissal of the indictment.[11]

———— ◆ ————

There are always readily identifiable people in politics who have perfectly good ideas as to what their party should do, and there are always enough political tigers around. However, the number of working politicians who will fall into both categories is far smaller than the number in either of them. Finally, of those who do have both the analytical ability and the requisite political instincts, not too many of them will also possess that attribute which is as essential as it is intangible, namely, the ability to render oneself acceptable.

Arthur Cromarty was one of those people who other people in the political game, if they had any perception at all, instinctively understood to be political down to his fingertips. He was one of those people who, if placed in a group of fifty other people, totally unknown to him, would, in due course, emerge with enough of them as his supporters to act as their leader, even if a majority of them did not care for him personally and said so. It goes without saying, of course, that a politician's capacity for manipulating politicians and non-politicians alike does not rest upon the plinth of his either being or being perceived as being a swell guy. It is not true that politicians who are unadmirable people or who are unpleasant, or both, do not finish first. That nice guys do not always finish last is beside the point.

As a matter of fact, people who for one reason or another wanted or felt obliged to deprecate him, often wondered out loud just how in the world Arthur Cromarty ever got to be county leader. But then, the mass of politicians are just like the mass of non-politicians in that they generally fail to distinguish between the qualities that we--unfortunately--learn as children inhere in the heroic and great--and therefore, mythic--leaders in our schoolbooks, and which, therefore, as we grow to adulthood we are unable to find in those in positions of leadership during our own lives, and the attributes which enable one to assume, i.e., to reach or obtain positions of leadership. Those of his competitors who were not totally enamored of him were not uncomfortable with him being characterized as crafty, or cagey, or even, on occasion, as "that poker player with a poker player's smile on his face."

However, neither Arthur Cromarty's ascension to, i.e., his winning of the leadership, nor his retention and optimum utilization of it was the consequence of his being or being perceived as being Jack Armstrong, the All-American Boy. Arthur Cromarty was not only a very astute politician, he was a very able one in what, after all, is the most basic and important sense of that term. He possessed the capacity to bring about the result he desired. He knew what to do and how to do it.

To attempt to analyze and then synthesize those qualities, abilities and instincts which, constituting the whole that is greater than the sum of its parts, are to be found in an effective political operator, the writer is satisfied, would be an exercise in futility, even for those in the trade who engage in the activity continually (which is not to say that we are not in great company when we do so, since the more intellectually inclined of the doers--and there are many of them--do think about such things); and for one to offer his analysis and synthesis as a working model for the edification of a non-politician would, as far as the writer is concerned, be a form of charlatanism, even though it is a perfectly understandable, worthwhile and harmless form of comparing notes among working politicians.

Now, there are--as there have always been--many, not in the trade, who, by way of political biography or commentary, do not hesitate to conceptualize, either explicitly or by implication, such a model. However, although it would be a form of dishonesty for a working politician with some analytical ability to do this, on the part of those not in the trade it is really to be condemned no more than to say that it is a form of fatuousness. Most working politicians would be content to acknowledge that in trying to solve the mystery, one is probably talking about just the right combination of the circumstances of time, place and the presence of and intercourse with other working politicians who, with varying degrees of motivation, tenacity and good fortune, are trying to be king of the mountain. The problem is that if one excludes surmise, gossip and speculation, which account for ninety five per cent of the data that observers feel is available to them, there is never any significant amount of reliable data available. This reflects the basic reality that most functionally significant activity is not conducted on a platform, in the newspapers, on a TV panel show or at a meeting. Most of it is the conduct of individuals who are operating as individuals upon other individuals in successions and series of sorties, each building upon the preceding ones and undertaken in connection with collateral movements. The only thing that politicians with sufficient intelligence and intellectual humility can say for sure is that some people are more successful than others in the game. The politician knows that issues for voters are created and do not just happen along; that the issues in intra-party warfare are just as important to the politician as the ones we read about, if not more so, notwithstanding that their creation and development are just as much man-made for political use as the ones we read about in editorials; and finally, that to a great extent, and beyond a certain point, no one politician can control political events. This is not because they are analytically deficient or intellectually lazy. It is simply that they know better than to draw inferences from irrelevancies, which they quite rightly respect as the turf of the political writer.

---◆---

While every political leader must, to a certain extent, pander or at least appear to be pandering to the defensively negative reactiveness of the mass of the working party--after all, they are his constituency--only a non-leader (and in the context of a political operation, a fool) would not concentrate on the necessity of being constructive. It is not only reasonable and right, it is necessary for a leader to demonstrate beyond peradventure of doubt a feeling of oneness with the herd in the various stages of its panic induced by something so unthinkable as the end of its monopoly of all public offices and other patronage--in other words, the end of the world. However, this is constructive and justifiable only to the extent necessary to achieve and maintain a sense of solidarity. He can say to intra-party gatherings until he's blue in the face, "I'm OK, You're OK, We're OK"; but, in any meaningful sense, this has to be taken to mean, "We'll be OK as long as we do something about the situation and do it real quick--and by the way, some of you won't like what we do, and some of you are going to get hurt."

Accordingly, the first thing Arthur Cromarty did after he became leader was to ask Lloyd Dodge to resign from the bench. The new leader's explanation for this request was a very nicely crafted statement of the level of civic responsibility which, it suggested, the Republican Party took for granted would obtain among all its officeholders. It read as follows: "I felt that the resignation of Judge Dodge, who occupies a position of high trust, was incumbent upon him, and that it was incumbent upon me as the new county leader to request his resignation."[12]

The free translation of this articulation of the party line is as follows: (1) Gee, Lloyd, it sure would have been an awfully decent thing
for you to have done had you resigned as soon as you were indicted,
simultaneously protesting your innocence but proclaiming even more
loudly that the confidence of our citizens in their judiciary is of far
greater importance than the fact that the career of an innocent person is being shattered for no other reason than it happens to be
suitable grist for the mill of the Democratic Party. (2) I know I have
no right to ask you to resign, but what can I do? They just elected
me leader, and if I don't ask you to resign, they'll put someone else in
who will."

(Judge Dodge refused to resign. However, he did make arrange-
ments with the county auditor to reimburse the county for the ex-
pense--$40 per day--of having an upstate judge come down to sit for
him.)[13]

On the face of it, Arthur Cromarty had a problem he could not
solve. After all, to say that something has to be done does not mean
that there is something that can be done. Once a three-headed
horse is out of the stable, in full public view, there is not much anyone can do to erase the image impressed upon the minds of all those
who have seen the beast. And you certainly can't pretend that the
horse never existed. This was highlighted by the editorials in *Newsday*, the bi-county daily newspaper for Nassau and suffolk Counties
which served as Suffolk's daily newspaper for local news. The essential message of these editorials was that it was hoped that our party
would interpret its losses on election day as a message from the
electorate that it had better clean house; that it could no longer put
forward for public office the same old hacks, to say nothing of those
who were tainted by association with the "rampant corruption" uncovered by the Special Prosecutor; and, that it should bear in mind
that the voters would be watching closely for affirmative signs of the
party's resolve to implement such changes as would entitle it once
more to the confidence of the county's citizens.

If one is not a politician, one does not have to be concerned
about the editorial simplisms and investigative reporting sideshows
that make up the political civic activity of the media. One is free to
turn off the TV or put down the newspaper with nothing more than
a sense of relief at being able to exercise his better judgment without

fear of the consequences. But it's different if one is a working politician. After all, all of us would prefer that what each of us is doing for his individual good be not be ascertained, divulged, examined or explained by outsiders; and even though our constitutional right to business privacy is unquestionably getting smaller and smaller all the time in the name of the political white horse called The Public Interest, most of us will not end up as grist for the mill of a investigative journalism performer or as a pretext for the aggrandizement of a politician. But a politician, following the same course of conduct as the rest of us--helping God help oneself--can never disregard the media. His basic feeling toward the media--as distinguished from what he is obliged to say about the media--is necessarily--and prudently--one of distrust and fear. It may constitute a resource if properly manipulated, and it may be shaped into a weapon; but like dynamite, it must be handled with extreme care. You can't be careless with a stick of TNT, and when handling it you can't take your safety for granted.

The problem, of course, was that while it is one thing to ferret out and demonstrate the fact of acts of corruption on the part of individuals, it is quite another to demonstrate that the party is not corrupt. After all, the only way you can do this is to have a period of time of quite some duration in which none of your officeholders is found to have been corrupt. Furthermore, unless one envisaged a total displacement of all those who were on the assembly line for entry positions and higher levels in the machinery of government, there could be no way in which one could demonstrate that we were not trying to foist "the same old gang" upon the public. The reason for this was that by association, if you had been a regular working politician in the party, you were necessarily a member of "the machine". If you were a member of "the machine", then you were certainly part of "the same old gang", and obviously you could not be categorized as being part of "a new breed of candidate" which these editorials made clear was required for the restoration of the party to "its former position of public confidence." The other side of this coin was that in between the debacle itself and the next biennial town and countywide elections, there was no real way in which a leader could demonstrate to the working politicians in the party that he had, in fact, made progress in the restoration of the party's strength. Except for the expected resolves to do the right thing, which were certain to be received or at least characterized as platitudes by those who either wanted an ironclad guarantee of the return of prosperity or by those who did not wish us well, there was nothing the Leader could do except to do the negative thing, which was to make it perfectly clear to the party that it would have to put forth the best possible candidates, and that it had to get out to the public the truth that the party had never condoned corruption, that it would have ferreted out through the normal course of operation of the District Attorney's Office those cases of actual corruption (as distinguished from the multitude of matters that had been demonstrated to have been not corruption at all or in many instances not even to have occurred), and that of course, the few rotten apples would have been discovered and gotten rid of.

Of course, there was a bright side of things for Arthur Cromarty. He had not become the Leader until we took our fall. In other words, his time in which to make good had not begun until we hit the floor.

Leaders do not normally have the reverence for The Leader that cardinals are said to have for the Pope. We are centuries beyond the time when a Pope had to worry about being murdered by his competitors. Political barons still commit regicide every day.

The impact this has on the leadership is to some degree a function of whether accession to and success and continuity in the leadership is part of a vocational plan or is really only an avocational activity. It's one thing if you're someone like W. Kingsland Macy, a person of wealth for whom the acquisition, exercise and maintenance of political leadership is engaged in simply for whatever amusement and ego-satisfaction it may afford. It's quite another, if by means of the leadership you're attempting to pull yourself up to a major bench by your own political bootstraps as your way of achieving financial security, professional recognition, and social status. Now, Arthur Cromarty was certainly in the latter group.

No matter what words of assurance and defiance Arthur Cromarty, the new county leader, may have uttered in order to engender the necessary positive feelings on the part of the troops that was required for their survival, he understood the gravity of the situation, but also, of course the opportunity afforded him by it, he having succeeded in capturing the leadership. For him, politics was something to engage in so that he could capitalize on his education and the fact of his law degree in order to make as nice as life for himself as he could.

--------◆--------

On January 12, 1960, the other two participants in the Kenson Merrill matter, Carl Hoffman and Arthur Calace, pleaded guilty to misdemeanor conspiracy counts of the Merrill indictments.[14]

On January 12th, Justice Markewich signed an order for the drawing of a second special grand jury, the present one having been reduced from its full complement of twenty-three members when it was impaneled in June, 1956, to seventeen, only one above the minimum membership required by law, and those who were left having served for three and one-half years. The special prosecutor announced, "The new jurors will take up new investigations which I cannot disclose." The old grand jury had enough strength left, however, to issue a presentment criticizing the former Republican administration of Huntington for permitting building inspectors to act as real estate brokers. Although the grand jury acknowledged that it was unable to determine that any crime had been committed in the one instance of such activity it had uncovered, it wanted to make clear that it felt that such a practice "opens a dangerous channel of corruption."[15]

On January 18th, the body of Kenson D. Merrill, an apparent suicide, was discovered.[16]

On January 25th, the Extraordinary Special and Trial Term grand jury handed up superseding indictments against Judge Dodge, Tom Keegan and Kenneth Leeds, which added Paul Greene, a former partner of Judge Dodge, as a defendant.[17]

On February 1st, the Governor, in his annual budget message to the Legislature, recommended $115,000 for the Suffolk County investigation. The Special Prosecutor had requested $195,000.[18]

On February 16th, Carl Hoffman and Arthur Calace were each fined $500 and given suspended three-month jail terms for their involvement with the late Kenson Merrill in the corruption of Brookhaven zoning matters, Justice Markewich noting that Merrill had been the prime mover.[19]

On April 28th, the Court of Appeals affirmed John Britting's convictions on the misdemeanor count of conspiracy to pervert and obstruct justice and the due administration of law, and on the nine felony counts of asking for or receiving bribes. However, it found that the charges against him on the nine felony counts of taking unlawful fees and the five misdemeanor counts of taking illegal fees were merged into the charges of bribery involving the identical facts. "In reality," the Court of Appeals concluded, "they amount to duplicate convictions, for the same offense and, as such, they are reversed and the counts dismissed."[20]

On May 10th, Rudolph Hahn, a highway foreman for the town of Brookhaven, who formerly had been engaged in selling road materials to a number of towns, villages and the State Department of Public Works, and David Hulsberg, an electrical assembler for Sperry Gyroscope Company, who formerly had been a truck contractor, were jointly indicted by the Extraordinary Special and Trial Term grand jury for presenting fraudulent claims and obtaining the proceeds of fraudulent claims. Mr. Hahn was the subject of another indictment charging him with fourteen counts of third-degree forgery. The substance of both indictments was that the defendants had charged $10,000 for the delivery of $5,000 worth of material to the Village of Babylon in 1956. The indictments were of no particular relevance to corruption. However, they gave the special prosecutor the opportunity to engage in a Shapiro-like stump speech in the courtroom. Upon the handing up of the indictments, Mr. Silberling explained that the failure of governmental agencies in Suffolk County not to protect themselves against such activities was common. He said that an analysis of one seventeen-day period "in one village has only scratched the surface of the systematic thievery." He promised that the investigation would be continued.

The regular grand jury declined to indict Mr. Silberling and three of his investigators, who had been charged with breaking and entering on the occasion of their serving search warrants upon Mr. Hulsberg.[21] What functional purpose the special prosecutor thought the personal presence on such an errand of a special assistant attorney general might serve, apart from any publicity it might produce for his personal crusade against evil, is a mystery that was never solved.

———— ◆ ————

In all, there were five indictments involving Judge Dodge: one in which he, Tom Keegan and Paul Greene were the defendants; one in which Judge Dodge was the sole defendant; two in which Judge Dodge and the real estate broker, Kenneth Leeds, were defendants; and one in which Kenneth Leeds was the sole defendant. The defendants had all moved for dismissal of the indictments. On May 26th, the Appellate Division voted unanimously to dismiss three of the counts of the indictment referable to Dodge, Keegan and Greene; and by a vote of three to two voted to deny the motions as to the balance of that indictment and as to the other indictments.[22]

On June 1st, Justice Markewich declined to disqualify himself from presiding at the trial of Judge Dodge. He had been requested to do so by Jim Fallon, Judge Dodge's attorney, upon the ground that Justice Markewich was a life-long friend of Judge Dodge's father, Wiliam C. Dodge, who had been a District Attorney of New York County.[23]

———— ◆ ————

On June 8th, consequent to the Court of Appeals' dismissal in April of duplicative counts against him, Britting was resentenced, from 2½-5 years to 1-2 years in state prison.[24]

———— ◆ ————

On July 5th, the State Civil Service Commission issued a report covering the period 1951-1959 which cited evidence of fraud in the examination papers of seventy candidates for positions in various town and village police departments in the county between 1953 and 1957. According to the report, it appeared that in some cases, incorrect answers had been corrected by someone other than the person taking the examination; and there were also instances of completely new answer sheets being substituted for the ones filled out by the candidates. The report further stated that there were thirty-three police officers appointed on the basis of these examinations, all of whom were still in the employ of their respective police departments.[25]

Tommy Calandrillo, our Commissioner of Jurors, had been the Executive Secretary of the Suffolk County Civil Service Commissioner during the entire period referable to the suspect examination papers. When he was questioned about the changes by the State Civil Service Commission, he had declined to answer, on advice of counsel. The day after the issuance of the State Civil Service Commission's report, Tommy suspended himself without pay from his position as Commissioner of Jurors. He asserted that he was ready to testify, and intended to return to his job as Commissioner of Jurors as soon as he was "cleared of these vicious rumors."[26]

The Special Prosecutor announced that he was going to start an investigation of the matter. District Attorney John Cohalan said the same thing. The Special Prosecutor countered with a reminder that he had a mandate from Governor Rockefeller to investigate corruption in the county.[27] However, the bell had now tolled for the scandals investigation.

It had been apparent from the nature of the indictments against Hahn and Hulsberg for bilking the Village of Babylon, from the Special Prosecutor's intrusion into the service of search warrants, and from the retrogression, in his stump speech which accompanied the handing up of those indictments, in which he was forced to rely on the political charge of laxness rather than that of corruption, that he had nowhere else to go for new indictments against public officials. Consequently, the Governor apparently must have concluded that it was now safe enough to start the shutting down of the special inquiry, for on July 11th, the Attorney General designated John Cohalan as the official to conduct the investigation of the alleged civil service examination irregularities.[28]

———— • ————

On July 20th, the Appellate Division unanimously reversed the convictions of John Hulsen and Jimmy Weber, and granted them a new trial. The Court said:

In our opinion it was highly prejudicial error to permit the admission into evidence of the 19 supplemental wire-tap records and transcripts of the series of telephone conversations between the defendants, and between them and others, during the period September 27, 1957 to October 23, 1957 . . . . Such conversations occurred after the commission of the crimes charged; the conversations related to collateral matters and to independent transactions and events wholly unconnected with any of the offenses set forth in the indictment; and the conversations had no logical reference to any of such offenses and did not prove or tend to prove defendants' guilt with respect to any of them. The nature of the contents of said wire-tap records and transcripts was such as to unduly prejudice the minds of the jurors by reason of other conduct by defendants which had nothing at all to do with the present case. We deem this error most prejudicial in the light of the prosecutor's allusions, both in his jury opening and summation, to the nature of these telephone conversations as reflected in said wire-tap records and transcripts. Such error requires a new trial, as a matter of law. We have not considered any of the other grounds of alleged error.[29]

Notes

1. Byron Porterfield, "G.O.P. Loses Rule of Suffolk Board," *New York Times*, November 4, 1959.
2. Editorial, "And Outside This City," ibid., November 5, 1959.
3. Byron Porterfield, "Republican Chief in Suffolk to Quit," ibid., November 7, 1959.
4. Byron Porterfield, "Suffolk G.O.P. Split in Fight on Leader," ibid., November 12, 1959.
5. "Suffolk's Sheriff Offers Ethics Code," ibid. November 13, 1959.

6. Byron Porterfield, "Suffolk G.O.P. Splits In Fight on Leader," ibid., November 12, 1959.

7. Ibid.

8. "Cromarty Succeeds Hughes as Suffolk Republican Leader," *Long Islander*, December 10, 1959.

9. *People v. Britting*, 9 A.D. 2d 897.

10. Byron Porterfield, "Suffolk Inquiry Accuses Company," *New York Times*, December 11, 1959

11. "Suffolk Charges Dismissed For 2," ibid., December 15, 1959.

12. "Indicted L.I. Judge Refuses to Resign," ibid., December 15, 1959.

13. Ibid.

14. "Banker Pleads Guilty," *New York Times*, January 12, 1960.

15. Byron Porterfield, "2D Jury Ordered in L.I. 'Scandals'," ibid., January 13, 1960.

16. "Ex-Town Aide Found Dead in his L.I. Home," ibid., January 19, 1960.

17. "Suffolk Grand Jury Indicts Judge Again In Zoning Scandal," ibid., January 26, 1960.

18. "'Little F.B.I.' Asked as Unit Under Division of State Police," ibid., February 2, 1960.

19. Byron Porterfield, "2 In Suffolk Fined in Zoning Racket," ibid., February 17, 1960.

20. *People v. Britting*, 8 N.Y.2d 771.

21. Byron Porterfield, "Two Men Indicted in L.I. Road Fraud," *New York Times*, May 11, 1960.

22. *People v. Dodge*, 10 A.D. 2nd 995

23. "Markewich to Hear Judge Dodge Case," *New York Times*, June 1, 1960.

24. "L.I. Ex-Legislator Wins Reduced Term," ibid., June 9, 1960.

25. "Test Frauds Laid to Suffolk Police," ibid., July 7, 1960.

26. "Another Inquiry Due on L.I. Police Tests," ibid., July 8, 1960.

27. Ibid.

28. "Police Inquiry Head Named in Suffolk," *New York Times*, July 12, 1960.

29. *People v. Hulsen and Weber*, 11 A.D. 2d 816, affirmed 9 N.Y.2d 730.

Chapter 10

The joint indictment against Judge Dodge and his two former partners contained nineteen felony counts charging them with the subornation of perjury in the first degree, and one count charging them with the misdemeanor of conspiracy to suborn perjury in the first degree. In his opening to the jury in the trial, the Special Prosecutor denounced the defendants for having "made a shambles" of the Town of Brookhaven's zoning ordinance by the criminal acts with which they were charged and which the State would establish they had committed.[1] Three of the felony counts had already been dismissed by the Appellate Division in May.[2] During the trial, two more of the felony counts were dismissed by Justice Markewich, and eleven of the remaining fourteen counts of subornation of perjury were reduced to charges of attempts to suborn perjury. As finally submitted to the jury by the trial court, the case against the defendants consisted of the one misdemeanor count of conspiracy, three felony counts of subornation of perjury in the first degree, and eleven felony counts of attempted subornation of perjury in the first degree.[3]

On July 29th, the defendants were found not guilty of all the felony counts, but guilty of the one misdemeanor count. The Special Prosecutor noted for the benefit of the press that the conviction involved moral turpitude; and that every evening, wrote to Governor Rockefeller notifying him of the conviction. Upon the rendering of the verdict, County Executive H. Lee Dennison declared that he would ask the Board of Supervisors for a resolution calling for the removal of Judge Dodge.[4]

Judge Dodge's conviction did not automatically result in his loss of office. He had to be removed from the bench. The Governor was the only person who could institute removal proceedings against him. He could do this by referring the matter to the State Senate, which could remove the judge by a two-thirds vote. The Senate being in recess until January, a referral to that body before then would require the Governor to call a special session of the Senate. The Governor could also refer the matter to the Court on the Judiciary, a special six-judge Court created in 1947 for the specific purpose of hearing charges against sitting judges.[5]

On August 1st, the Board of Supervisors unanimously petitioned the Governor "to institute immediate removal proceedings."[6]

———◦◦———

On August 5th, the Administrator of the State Judicial Conference announced that Judge Dodge had informed the Conference that he would neither serve nor draw pay as county judge pending the outcome of his appeal.[7]

———◦◦———

On September 12th, Judge Dodge, Tom Keegan and Paul Greene appeared for sentencing. Keegan and Green each received suspended three-month sentences, a special condition of their probation being that they not practice law pending the outcome of any disciplinary action that might be instituted against them consequent to their convictions. Upon Judge Dodge being called for sentence, Justice Markewich, instead of proceeding to the imposition of a sentence, asked Dodge to end his suspension by resigning from the bench. When Dodge refused to do this, Markewich did not impose sentence; he simply told Dodge to think it over for a day.[8]

The next day, Justice Markewich again requested that Dodge resign forthwith, and when dodge again declined to do so, Markewich proclaimed, "Ever since the trial, this man has been in a dream world with all those around him telling him that he has been the victim of persecution. He needs a good stiff jolt. He needs to be insulated from this audience which surrounds him." He then revoked Judge Dodge's bail, and continued the imposition of sentence to October 3rd, effectually sentencing Judge Dodge to twenty-one days in jail for refusing to resign from the bench. After thus pioneering a new reason to revoke a defendant's bail, Justice Markewich ordered the forwarding of the proceedings to the Governor so that the Governor could without delay convene the State Senate in special session for the institution of removal proceedings against Judge Dodge. The jurist explained his action, manifesting again the deep reverence for the right of an accused to defend himself in general, which he had exhibited on the sentencing of John Britting, and also, on this occasion, his recognition of a defendant's right to do battle with a prosecutor:

> Judge Dodge's testimony alone under cross-examination was enough to damn him. His testimony was evasive and he displayed a slick smoothness and suddenness in averting answer. In my view, if he sits again as judge, it will constitute an affront to the community, the bar, and the entire system of our courts.[9]

In short, no matter what the question was or how it was phrased, the defendant had an ethical obligation to give the prosecutor the answer he wanted, which apparently was also the answer that Justice Markewich wanted.

The Special Prosecutor joined in tying the tin can on the cat's tail by demanding that Dodge be forced to return the salary he had drawn since his indictment.[10]

Judge Dodge obtained a writ of habeas corpus, seeking to obtain his release on the ground that he was being illegally imprisoned. However, the writ was dismissed by the Supreme Court Justice before whom it was returnable at a regular Special Term of the Supreme Court, upon the ground that he was without jurisdiction to act in matters solely within the province of the Justice presiding at Extraordinary Term, i.e., the revoking of a defendant's bail and the scheduling of a date for sentencing.[11] Undeterred, Jim Fallon, Dodge's attorney, brought a proceeding against Justice Markewich in the Appellate Division, in which he sought an order in the nature of *mandamus* compelling Justice Markewich to immediately pronounce sentence upon the defendant. The Appellate Division granted the motion to dismiss the petition upon the ground that it failed to state facts sufficient to entitle the petitioner to relief, i.e., that there was no basis in law for such an order. However, the Court granted the motion "without prejudice to renewal"; and then ended its opinion with the following sentence: "It appears that the sentencing of petitioner is definitely fixed for October 3, 1960."[12]

On September 20th, Robert McCrate, Counsel to the Governor, wrote to Justice Markewich, advising him of that which he already knew, *viz.*, that it would be premature for the Governor to issue a call for a special session of the State Senate to consider removal of Judge Dodge in view of the fact that there was as yet no final disposition of the proceedings against the judge; and, that for the same reason, the Court on the Judiciary would not be convening presently to consider the matter.[13]

When Judge Dodge was brought from the county jail for sentencing on October 3rd, Justice Markewich noted that Governor Rockefeller had chosen not to act on the court's recommendation that the State Senate be convened for removal proceedings against Judge Dodge, notwithstanding the fact that "I am morally certain that Dodge's testimony in this case marks him as unfit to hold the office of judge." He then sentenced Judge Dodge to six months in the county jail, freed him on $1,000 bail until October 17th, when he was to start his imprisonment.[14]

In the meantime, Lloyd Dodge's former partners, Keegan and Greene, once they had been sentenced on September 12th, were in a position to apply for a certificates of reasonable doubt. The Special Prosecutor did not argue or submit a brief on the merits of their applications, opposing them solely upon the ground that a certificate should not issue because, the sentences having been suspended, there was no judgment. Since in each case the Extraordinary Trial and Special Term had entered a judgment of imprisonment of three months, the execution of which was suspended, the Court hearing the applications summarily rejected that argument. On the merits, Mr. Justice Robinson concluded that at least one of the errors claimed to justify the issuance of the certificate, namely that the instructions to the jury in connection with questions it had raised concerning conspiracy were insufficient and confusing, was sufficient to raise a doubt as to whether the convictions would stand on appeal; and he granted the writ.[15]

Following his sentencing on October 3rd, Lloyd Dodge applied for a certificate of reasonable doubt. Mr. Justice Hogan opened his discussion of the application with an oblique reference to Judge Dodge's 21-day incarceration for refusing to resign:

> A certificate of reasonable doubt already has been issued by Mr. Justice Robinson as to [Dodge's] co-defendants, Mr. Greene and Mr. Keegan, based upon the likelihood that the jury was confused by certain portions of the presiding Justice's charge. That finding by Justice Robinson, which this Court also adopts, would have applied, of course, to this defendant as well, if his application could have been submitted at that time.[16]

Justice Hogan then went on to discuss additional grounds for reason to doubt that the conviction would be sustained on appeal, and directed the issuance of the certificate.

———— ◆ ————

In the normal course of events, the trial of Kenneth Leeds, the real estate operator who had been indicted with Dodge, Keegan and Greene, which had been severed from that of his co-defendants, would have followed theirs. Following their conviction, Leeds moved in the Appellate Division for a stay of his trial, it being his obvious hope that in the event of a reversal of the convictions of his co-defendants, he could avoid the perils of going to trial himself, particularly that of a felony conviction. However, on September 8th, the Appellate Division denied his motion;[17] and so, on September 13th, when Keegan and Greene were sentenced, Leeds, in order to preclude the possibility of a felony conviction after a trial, pleaded guilty to the same misdemeanor which the jury had found Dodge, Green and Keegan guilty of, conspiracy to commit perjury in the first degree, in satisfaction of all counts of the indictment against him. On October 25th, he was sentenced to a fine of $500.[18]

———————— ◆ ————————

On November 14th, three Suffolk County policemen were arraigned on indictments handed up by a special grand jury impaneled by the District Attorney. Each policeman was charged with one count of first degree perjury for identifying to the grand jury as their own handwriting on their test papers handwriting which had been identified for the grand jury police handwriting experts as not being theirs.[19]

On November 21st, Rudolph Hahn, one of the two men indicted for submitting fraudulent bills to the Village Babylon in 1956, was fined $500 and given a nine-month sentence, suspended on condition of his repayment to the village of Babylon of the sum of $2,598, the amount apparently agreed upon as the overpayment involved in the transactions which gave rise to the multi-felony count indictments handed down against him and David Hulsberg in May.[20]

On December 19th, Tommy Calandrillo pleaded innocent to a 35-felony-count indictment charging him with forgery, injury to records, and perjury, for changing the answers on seven policemen's tests and then lying about it to the grand jury.[21]

On March 2, 1961, the Court of Appeals affirmed the Appellate Divison's reversal of the conviction of John Hulsen and Jimmy Weber.[22]

———————— ◆ ————————

On March 3rd, the Appellate Division reversed the Dodge-Keegan-Greene convictions of conspiracy to suborn perjury in the first degree on the law and the facts, and dismissed the indictment underlying them.[23]

The indictment was based upon eighteen petitions for relief from changes in building lot requirements of the Town of Brookhaven Building Zone Ordinance which had been enacted on April 18, 1954, which petitions had been prepared by the law firm of Dodge, Keegan and Greene. The conspiracy with which the defendants had been charged was to suborn perjury on the part of their clients with respect to material matters in connection with the petitions. The material matters were the asserted requirements of the ordinance that petitioners for the relief sought by the defendants' clients had owned their land prior to April 18, 1954, that they had expended money in its development prior to that date, and that they would continue to develop the land. The perjury which the defendants were charged with conspiring to suborn was the false statements of their clients to the effect that they met those requirements.[24]

Presiding Justice Nolan analyzed the the language of the May 25, 1954 amendment to the ordinance which created the right to seek the relief requested by the defendants' clients, the legislative history of that amendment, and the relevant--and well-settled--law, and found as follows:

> It is clear . . . that it was not necessary for property owners who sought relief [pursuant to the amendment] to state in their petitions that they had purchased their land in reliance upon the provisions of the ordinance in existence prior to April 18, 1954, or had expended money in developing the land and would continue to develop it. Neither was it necessary for them to establish such facts in order to obtain relief.
>
> We are unable to say, however, that such statements, if made, would have been immaterial as a matter of law. The test is whether such statements, if made, could properly have influenced the Town Board upon any question which was before it for determination [case citations]. . . and we cannot say that the Town Board could not properly have taken into consideration, in determining whether to grant relief, the fact that land had been purchased and money had been expended on it in reliance on the provision of the old ordinance, even though proof of such facts was not necessary. It was for the jury to determine, on appropriate instructions, whether the

statements alleged in the indictments, were made, and if they were made whether they were material [case citation].

The jury were charged that it was their function to determine both questions, but the instructions given them practically precluded a determination that the statements which defendants were accused of conspiring to induce their clients to make, were not material . . . .

Under these instructions, the jury must have understood that [the amendment] required an applicant for relief from the zoning regulations to establish that he had purchased his land and spend money developing it prior to April 18, 1954, and that if such statements were contained in the petitions they were material, in spite of the instruction also given that it was for them to determine as an issue of fact whether the statements in the petitions were or were not material. In our opinion, the charge on this issue was erroneous and requires reversal.

Whether a new trial should be directed or whether the indictment should be dismissed, depends on whether the evidence was sufficient to establish beyond a reasonable doubt that defendants conspired to induce their clients to make the false statements alleged in the indictment. We have concluded that it was not.

The prosecutor attempted to establish the conspiracy charged against defendants by circumstantial evidence, asserting that a corrupt agreement could be inferred from the evidence adduced on the substantive counts, upon which the defendants were found not guilty. It was the prosecutor's theory that the conspiracy was established by proof that on behalf of their clients defendants prepared and presented 18 petitions for relief which were similar in form and content, and which contained false statements that the petitioners had purchased their property in reliance on the Zoning Ordinance in existence prior to April 18, 1954, and had expended large sums of money in developing the land and would continue to develop the land.[25]

Justice Nolan then proceeded to analyze the eighteen petitions.

He found that one of the petitions did state that the property had been purchased in reliance on the ordinance as it existed prior to the change on April 18, 1954; and, that it had been established that the property was purchased prior to that date. It found that a second petition stated that the owner had acted in reliance upon the ordinance as it existed prior to the change April, 1954; and, that it had been conceded that a portion of the property had been purchased prior to April, 1954. It found that a third petition stated that the property had been purchased sometime prior to the change in the ordinance, in reliance upon the ordinance as it existed prior to April, 1954; and, that these statements were false, but that the evidence with respect to that petition was insufficient to establish a conspiracy between the defendants to induce the false statements.[26]

With respect to the remaining fifteen petitions, which he described as being "practically identical in form and content," Justice Nolan found as follows:

No date of purchase of any of the land was stated in any of these 15 petitions, nor did any of these petitioners state that he purchased the land in reliance upon the ordinance in existence prior to April 18, 1954. No petition stated that money had been expended on the development of the land involved, except that in one instance the petitioner stated that he had expended money in the development of the "area" relying on the previous zoning ordinance. Neither did the petitions state that petitioners would continue to develop the land. . . .[27]

Justice Nolan would conclude:

Actually, what was established was, not that the peti-

tions contained the statements alleged in the indictment to have been included in them, but that they did
not contain such statements. . . .

. . .

. . . It is to be noted that with respect to these
same petitions the jury did not find the evidence sufficient to establish the charges of subornation or attempted subornation of perjury submitted to them
under other counts of the indictment. In our opinion
the evidence was also insufficient to establish the
conspiracy of which defendants were convicted.[28]

Justices Kleinfeld, Christ and Pette concurred with Justice Nolan.
Justice Beldock concurred in the result.

The day after the Appellate Division handed down its decision,
Judge Dodge's attorney announced that he would move to dismiss
the other two indictments against his client, presumably on the basis
that the Appellate Division's opinion dealt a fatal blow to their legal
and factual sufficiency.[29]

———————— • ————————

On April 14th, on the recommendation of the Attorney General,
John Hulsen, the conviction of whom and Jimmy Weber of attempted extortion, coercion and conspiracy had been reversed by the Appellate Division, which ordered a new trial, was permitted to plead
to a reduced charge of coercion; received a suspended sentence of
three months in the county jail and a fine of $500; and was permitted
to exonerate Jimmy, i.e., to take full blame for the attempted extortion, which would enable Jimmy to regain his membership in the Bar,
which had ceased upon his conviction of a felony.[30] In his recommendation of this disposition of the matter, Attorney General
Lefkowitz observed that the defendant Hulsen "has acknowledged
his guilt and I believe his political power is gone."[31]

Also on April 14th, the charges against Judge Dodge were dismissed by Justice Markewich upon the recommendation of the Attorney General consequent to Judge Dodge's resignation.[32] (The *Long
Islander* quoted Arthur Cromarty as saying that he was "gratified" by

the resignation. It quoted him further: "It is my belief that this is not simply a question of any innocence or guilt, but that there should be no cloud of any sort over a judicial office." The Democratic county leader, Adrian Mason, was equally gratified, asserting that Judge Dodge had "lost his usefulness and trust as a public servant."[33])

———— ◆ ————

On June 12th, the Appellate Division reversed the conviction of J. Milford Kirkup, Jr., notwithstanding its affirmance of the findings of fact below, because the "misconduct of the prosecutor [Mr. Silberling], coupled with the sequence of the events [set forth in the Court's opinion], was so prejudicial as to deprive the defendant of a fair trial." The Appellate Division noted that "[t]he Trial Court [Justice Markewich] did "all in its power to minimize any possible mischief."[34]

On June 28th, on consent of the District Attorney's office, Justice Markewich imposed a suspended sentence on Mr. Kirkup, upon the latter's plea to one misdemeanor count in satisfaction of his multicount indictment, noting that there was never any consideration received for Kirkup's doing a favor for his friend, the druggist whom he enabled to purchase drugs at institional prices; and, that the only reason he had originally sentenced Kirkup to a jail term was because he had testified falsely at his trial.[35]

Also on June 28th, Justice Markewich officially closed the Suffolk County Scandals Investigations.[36]

———— ◆ ————

On July 7th, Tommy Calandrillo would be permitted to plead guilty to one count of perjury in the second degree, a misdemeanor, in satisfaction of the 35 felony-count indictment charging him with forgery, injury to records, and perjury, for which he was sentenced to three months in the county jail by County Judge Ellsworth N. Lawrence, visiting from upstate Franklin County.

John Cohalan, in the course of recommending acceptance of the plea, noted that the defendant had never requested or accepted money from the police officers; and, "that he had listened unwisely to the blandishments of the siren song of an older man, in the hope presumably of political preferment." Tommy was a resident of Huntington. The *Long Islander* noted that the District Attorney's allusion to "an older man" was a reference to "former Huntington Republican Leader John H. Hulsen."[37]

Notes

1. "Zoning Trial Opens For Suffolk Judge," *New York Times*, June 30, 1960.
2. *People v. Dodge, Greene and Keegan*, 10 A.D. 2d 995.
3. *People v. Dodge*, 12 A.D. 2d 353.
4. "L.I. Judge Guilty in Zoning Fraud," *New York Times*, July 30, 1960.
5. "2 Actions Possible," ibid.
6. "Action to Oust Convicted Judge In Suffolk Is Urged on Governor," *New York Times*, August 2, 1960.
7. "Judge Foregoes Pay," ibid., August 6, 1960.
8. Byron Porterfield, "Convicted Judge Sent to L.I. Jail," ibid., September 14, 1960.
9. Ibid.
10. Ibid.
11. "Judge Jailed on L.I. Fails to Win Writ," *New York Times*, September 15, 1960.
12. *Matter of Dodge, pet (Markewich, res)*, N.Y.L.J., September 26, 1960, App. Div., p. 13, Col. 6.
13. "No Action on Judge," *New York Times*, September 21, 1960.
14. Byron Porterfield, "Judge Sentenced in Suffolk Fraud," ibid., October 4, 1960.
15. *People, &c., v. Dodge et al.* (Greene), N.Y.L.J., September 28, 1960, at 15 col 4 (Sup. Ct. Nassau County); (Keegan), at 15, col 5.
16. *People v. Dodge*, 208 N.Y.S. 2d 817, 818 (Sup. Ct., Suffolk County)
17. *People v. Leeds*, 11 A.D. 2d.
18. "Land Dealer Fined in Suffolk Inquiry," *New York Times*, October 26, 1960

19. Byron Porterfieled, "Suffolk Indicts 3 Over Police Tests," ibid., November 15, 1960.

20. "L.I. Contractor Fined," ibid., November 22, 1960.

21. "Suffolk Indicts Chief of Jurors," ibid., December 20, 1960.

22. *People v. Hulsen and Weber,* 9 A.D. 2d 730

23. *People v. Dodge,* 12 A.D. 2d 353.

24. *Id.*

25. *Id.,* at 360-361.

26. *Id.* at 361-362.

27. *Id.* at 362-363.

28. *Id.* at 364.

29. "L.I. Judge to Seek to Clear His Name," *New York Times,* March 5, 1961.

30. Byron Porterfield, "2 Suffolk Cases Settled By Court," ibid., April 15, 1961.

31. "Hulsen Pleads Guilty to Coercion; Weber Exonerated," *Long Islander,* April 20, 1961.

32. Byron Porterfield, "2 Suffolk Cases Settled By Court," *New York Times,* April 15, 1961.

33. "Dodge Resigns; Markewich Drops Pending Charges," *Long Islander,* April 20, 1961.

34. *People v. Kirkup,* 216 N.Y.S. 2nd 750 (App. Div., Second Department 1961)

35. "Suffolk Probe Ends; Judge Dismisses Juries," *Long Islander,* June 29, 1961.

36. Ibid.

37. "Calandrillo Begins 90-Day Sentence on Perjury Charge," *Long Islander,* July 13, 1961

CPSIA information can be obtained
at www.ICGtesting.com
Printed in the USA
BVHW041107250719
554363BV00017B/1792/P